Campbell's®
Simple 1-2-3
Recipes

Publications International, Ltd.

Favorite Brand Name Recipes at www.fbnr.com

Photography on pages 5, 14, 17, 18, 24, 25, 38, 39, 40, 41, 91, 119, 122, 123, 133, 135, 139, 145, 150, and 152 by Stephen Hamilton Photographics, Inc., Chicago.
Ingredient photography by Shaughnessy MacDonald, Inc.

Pictured on the front cover: Swiss Vegetable Bake *(page 105).*
Pictured on the back cover (clockwise from top): Shrimp & Corn Chowder with Sun-Dried Tomatoes *(page 39)*, Chicken Nacho Tacos *(page 91)* and Warm Spinach Dip *(page 25).*

ISBN-13: 978-1-4127-2370-1
ISBN-10: 1-4127-2370-1

Manufactured in China.

8 7 6 5 4 3 2 1

Microwave Cooking: Microwave ovens vary in wattage. Use the cooking times as guidelines and check for doneness before adding more time.

Preparation/Cooking Times: Preparation times are based on the approximate amount of time required to assemble the recipe before cooking, baking, chilling or serving. These times include preparation steps such as measuring, chopping and mixing. The fact that some preparations and cooking can be done simultaneously is taken into account. Preparation of optional ingredients and serving suggestions is not included.

Contents

Appetizers & Snacks

Layered Pizza Dip

1 cup part-skim ricotta cheese

½ cup chopped pepperoni

1 cup shredded mozzarella cheese (4 ounces)

1 cup Prego® Pasta Sauce, any variety

Pepperidge Farm® Garlic Bread, any variety, heated according to package directions **or** Pepperidge Farm® Crackers, any variety

START TO FINISH: 30 minutes

Prepping: 10 minutes
Baking: 15 minutes
Cooling: 5 minutes

1. Spread the ricotta cheese in an even layer in a 9-inch pie plate. Top with ¼ **cup** of the pepperoni and ½ **cup** mozzarella cheese. Carefully spread the pasta sauce over the cheese. Sprinkle with the remaining pepperoni and mozzarella cheese.

2. Bake at 375°F. for 15 minutes or until hot. Let cool for 5 minutes.

3. Serve with the garlic bread or crackers for dipping.

Makes: About 3 cups

Easy Substitution Tip: Substitute or add any of the following toppings for the pepperoni: Sliced pitted olives, sliced mushrooms, chopped sweet peppers **or** chopped onions.

1¾ cups Prego® Traditional
  Pasta Sauce
¼ cup dry red wine
1 cup shredded mozzarella
  cheese (4 ounces)

Suggested Dippers: Warm
Pepperidge Farm® Garlic
Bread, cut into cubes,
meatballs, sliced cooked
Italian pork sausage, breaded
mozzarella sticks **and/or**
whole mushrooms

Italiano Fondue

START TO FINISH: 20 minutes

Prepping: 5 minutes
Cooking: 10 minutes
Standing: 5 minutes

1. Mix the pasta sauce and wine in a 1-quart saucepan. Bring to a boil over medium heat, stirring often. Cook for 5 minutes for the alcohol to evaporate.

2. Pour the sauce into a fondue pot or slow cooker. Stir in the cheese. Let stand for 5 minutes for cheese to melt slightly.

3. Serve warm with *Suggested Dippers*.

Makes: 2 cups

Appetizers & Snacks

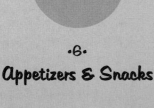

Fiesta Cilantro Fondue

START TO FINISH: 15 minutes

Prepping: 5 minutes
Cooking: 10 minutes

1. Mix the soup and beer in a 1-quart saucepan. Bring to a boil over medium heat. Stir in the salsa and the cheese. Heat through until the cheese melts, stirring occasionally.

2. Pour the sauce into a fondue pot or slow cooker.

3. Serve warm with *Suggested Dippers*.

Makes: 2 cups

1 can (10¾ ounces) Campbell's® Condensed Creamy Chicken Verde Soup
¼ cup beer
½ cup Pace® Cilantro Chunky Salsa
2 cups shredded Cheddar cheese (8 ounces)

Suggested Dippers: Assorted Pepperidge Farm® Crackers, French bread cubes, cooked breaded chicken nuggets, steamed vegetables (asparagus spears, broccoli flowerets, red potato wedges) **and/or** tortilla chips

Appetizers & Snacks

1 loaf (about 1 pound) Italian bread, cut lengthwise
1 can (10¾ ounces) Campbell's® Condensed Cream of Mushroom Soup (Regular **or** 98% Fat Free)
¼ teaspoon garlic powder
¼ teaspoon Italian seasoning, crushed
1 small red pepper, chopped (about ½ cup)
2 medium green onions, chopped (about ¼ cup)
1 cup shredded mozzarella cheese (4 ounces)
1 tablespoon grated Parmesan cheese

Mushroom Mozzarella Bruschetta

START TO FINISH: 20 minutes

Prepping: 15 minutes
Baking: 5 minutes

1. Heat the oven to 400°F. Place the bread halves on a baking sheet. Bake for 5 minutes or until lightly toasted.

2. Mix the soup, garlic powder and Italian seasoning, pepper, green onions, mozzarella cheese and Parmesan cheese in a medium bowl. Spread the soup mixture over bread halves to within ¼ inch of edge.

3. Bake for 5 minutes or until hot. Cut each bread half into 12 slices.

Makes: 24 appetizers

Appetizers & Snacks

Walnut-Cheddar Ball

START TO FINISH: 2 hours 20 minutes

Prepping: 20 minutes
Refrigerating: 2 hours

1. Mix the cheese, walnuts, mayonnaise, green onion, mustard and Worcestershire in a 1½-quart bowl.

2. Mix the parsley and paprika on a piece of wax paper. Shape the cheese mixture into a ball, then roll in the parsley mixture to coat. Wrap in plastic wrap. Refrigerate for 2 hours or until firm.

3. Unwrap the cheese ball and place on a serving plate. Serve with the crackers.

Makes: 2 cups

2 cups shredded Cheddar cheese (8 ounces)
½ cup finely chopped walnuts
¼ cup mayonnaise
1 medium green onion, chopped (about 2 tablespoons)
1 tablespoon Dijon-style mustard
1 teaspoon Worcestershire sauce
¼ cup chopped fresh parsley
1 tablespoon paprika
Pepperidge Farm® Cracker Quartet or Cracker Trio Entertaining Collection Cracker Assortment

1 package (8 ounces) cream cheese, softened
1 can (10¾ ounces) Campbell's® Condensed Cream of Shrimp Soup
½ teaspoon Louisiana-style hot sauce
¼ cup finely chopped celery
1 tablespoon finely chopped onion
Assorted Pepperidge Farm® Crackers, chips **or** cut-up fresh vegetables

Shrimp Dip

START TO FINISH: 2 hours 5 minutes

Prepping: 5 minutes
Refrigerating: 2 hours

1. Stir the cheese in a medium bowl until it's smooth. Stir in the soup, hot sauce, celery and onion.

2. Refrigerate the mixture for 2 hours or until the flavors are blended.

3. Serve with the crackers, chips or vegetables for dipping.

Makes: 2¼ cups

Porcupine Meatballs

START TO FINISH: 35 minutes

Prepping: 15 minutes
Cooking: 20 minutes

1. Thoroughly mix the turkey, rice, egg, oregano, garlic powder and black pepper in a medium bowl.

2. Shape the mixture into 25 meatballs.

3. Heat the pasta sauce in a 12-inch skillet over medium-high heat. Add the meatballs in one layer. Heat to a boil. Reduce the heat to low. Cover and cook for 10 minutes or until meatballs are cooked through*.

Makes: 5 servings

The internal temperature of the meatballs should reach 160°F.

- 1 pound ground turkey
- 2 cups cooked brown **or** regular long-grain white rice
- 1 egg
- ¾ teaspoon dried oregano leaves, crushed
- ½ teaspoon garlic powder
- ¼ teaspoon ground black pepper
- 1 jar (1 pound 10 ounces) Prego® Traditional **or** Tomato, Basil & Garlic Pasta Sauce

1 package (9.5 ounces)
    Pepperidge Farm®
    Mozzarella & Monterey
    Jack Cheese Texas
    Toast
6 tablespoons Pace®
    Refried Beans
Pace® Chunky Salsa, any
    variety
Sour cream (optional)
Chopped green onions
    (optional)

Tex-Mex Toasts

START TO FINISH: 22 minutes

Prepping: 20 minutes
Baking: 2 minutes

1. Prepare the toast according to the package directions.

2. Spread **1 tablespoon** of the beans on each toast slice. Bake for 2 minutes more or until hot.

3. Top each toast slice with salsa, sour cream and green onions, if desired.

Makes: 6 servings

Cooking for a Crowd: Recipe may be doubled.

Appetizers & Snacks

Spicy Grilled Quesadillas

START TO FINISH: 17 minutes

Prepping: 10 minutes
Grilling: 5 minutes
Standing: 2 minutes

1. Put **4** of the tortillas on a work surface. Top each with ½ **cup** of the cheese, ¼ **cup** salsa, ¼ **cup** chicken and **2 tablespoons** green onions. Top with the remaining tortillas.

2. Lightly oil the grill rack and heat the grill to medium. Brush the tops of the quesadillas with some oil. Place the quesadillas oil-side down on the grill for 3 minutes. Brush the tops of the quesadillas with some oil and turn over. Grill for 2 minutes more or until lightly browned. Remove the quesadillas from the grill and let stand for 2 minutes.

3. Cut the quesadillas into wedges. Serve with the remaining salsa and sour cream.

Makes: 4 servings

8 flour tortillas (8-inch)
2 cups shredded Cheddar cheese (8 ounces)
1 jar (16 ounces) Pace® Chunky Salsa, any variety
1 cup diced cooked chicken
4 medium green onions, chopped (about ½ cup)
Vegetable oil
1 cup sour cream

1 cup mayonnaise
1 cup sour cream
1 can (14 ounces) artichoke hearts, drained and chopped
¼ cup chopped roasted sweet peppers
¼ cup grated Parmesan cheese
1 can (2.8 ounces) french fried onions (1⅓ cups)
Assorted Pepperidge Farm® Crackers

Hot Artichoke Dip

START TO FINISH: 40 minutes

Prepping: 10 minutes
Baking: 30 minutes

1. Heat the oven to 375°F. Mix the mayonnaise, sour cream, artichokes, peppers, cheese and ⅔ **cup** onions in 9-inch pie plate or 1-quart baking dish. Bake for 25 minutes or until hot.

2. Top with the remaining onions. Bake for 5 minutes more or until golden.

3. Serve with the crackers for dipping.

Makes: 3 cups

Grilled Bruschetta

START TO FINISH: 22 minutes

Prepping: 5 minutes
Marinating: 15 minutes
Grilling: 2 minutes

1. Stir the oil, vinegar, garlic, black pepper, parsley and tomatoes in a medium bowl. Let the mixture marinate for at least 15 minutes.

2. Lightly oil the grill rack and heat the grill to medium. Grill the toast slices for 2 minutes or until they're browned and heated through, turning once.

3. Divide the tomato mixture evenly among the toast slices. Serve immediately.

Makes: 8 servings

Omit garlic if using garlic Texas toast.

3 tablespoons olive oil
2 tablespoons red wine vinegar
2 cloves garlic, minced*
½ teaspoon cracked black pepper
2 tablespoons chopped fresh parsley **or** basil leaves
2 medium tomatoes, chopped (about 2 cups)
1 package (11.25 ounces) Pepperidge Farm® Parmesan **or** Garlic Texas Toast

Appetizers & Snacks

¼ cup light whipped cream cheese

4 slices Pepperidge Farm® Very Thin Wheat **or** White Bread, toasted

1 cup thinly sliced cucumber

¼ cup diced canned beets Fresh dill sprigs

Cheesy Vegetable Triangles

START TO FINISH: 15 minutes

Prepping: 15 minutes

1. Spread **about 1 tablespoon** of the cream cheese on each toast slice.

2. Divide the cucumber and beets among the toast slices.

3. Cut the sandwiches diagonally into quarters. Top each quarter with a dill sprig. Serve immediately.

Makes: 16 appetizers

Appetizers & Snacks

Salmon Bites

START TO FINISH: 15 minutes

Prepping: 15 minutes

1. Stir the mayonnaise and lemon juice in a medium bowl. Stir in the salmon.

2. Divide the tomato slices and salmon mixture among the toast slices and top with the red onion.

3. Cut the sandwiches diagonally into quarters. Serve immediately.

Makes: 16 appetizers

¼ **cup lowfat mayonnaise**
2 **teaspoons fresh lemon juice**
1 **can (about 6 ounces) white or pink salmon, drained and flaked**
1 **medium tomato, cut in half and thinly sliced**
4 **slices Pepperidge Farm® Very Thin Wheat or White Bread, toasted**
¼ **cup very thinly sliced red onion**

Appetizers & Snacks

¼ cup light cream cheese, softened

1 teaspoon chopped fresh cilantro

1 teaspoon fresh lime juice

4 slices Pepperidge Farm® Very Thin Wheat **or** White Bread, toasted

½ cup imitation crabmeat (surimi), broken into bite size pieces

Fresh cilantro sprigs

Appetizers & Snacks

Seafood & Cilantro Sandwiches

START TO FINISH: 20 minutes

Prepping: 20 minutes

1. Mix the cheese, cilantro and lime juice in a small bowl.

2. Spread **about 1 tablespoon** of the cheese mixture on each toast slice. Divide the crabmeat among the toast slices.

3. Cut the sandwiches diagonally into quarters. Top each quarter with a cilantro sprig. Serve immediately.

Makes: 16 appetizers

Sausage Stuffed Mushrooms

START TO FINISH: 35 minutes

Prepping: 25 minutes
Baking: 10 minutes

1. Remove the stems from the mushrooms. Chop enough stems to make **1 cup**. Brush the mushroom caps with the butter and set the caps topside down in a shallow baking pan.

2. Cook the sausage and mushroom stems in a 10-inch skillet over medium-high heat until the sausage is well browned, stirring to break up the meat. Stir in ½ **cup** of the picante sauce and bread crumbs. Spoon **about 1 tablespoon** of the sausage mixture into each mushroom cap.

3. Bake at 425°F. for 10 minutes or until hot and the sausage mixture reaches an internal temperature of 160°F. Top each mushroom with **1 teaspoon** of the remaining picante sauce and cilantro.

Makes: 24 appetizers

24 medium mushrooms
2 tablespoons butter, melted
¼ pound bulk pork sausage
1 cup Pace® Picante Sauce
½ cup dry bread crumbs
Chopped fresh cilantro or parsley

24 Reynolds® Foil Baking Cups (2½-inch)
1 can (15.5 ounces) Pace® Refried Beans
2 jars (11 ounces **each**) Pace® Chunky Salsa
3 medium avocados, peeled and chopped (about 1½ cups)
1½ cups shredded Cheddar cheese (6 ounces)
1½ cups sour cream
½ cup chopped fresh cilantro leaves
Bite-size tortilla chips

Single-Serve Southwest Dip Cups

START TO FINISH: 20 minutes

Prepping: 20 minutes

1. Place the foil cups on a serving platter.

2. Layer **about 1 tablespoon** each of the beans, salsa, avocado and cheese into **each** cup. Top each with a spoonful of sour cream and sprinkle with cilantro.

3. Serve with the chips for dipping.

Makes: 24 servings

Appetizers & Snacks

Caponata Appetizers

START TO FINISH: 1 hour

Prepping: 15 minutes
Cooking: 45 minutes

1. Heat the oil in a 6-quart saucepot over medium-high heat. Add the eggplant, onion, pepper and garlic and cook for 10 minutes or until the eggplant begins to soften.

2. Stir in the soup and water and heat the mixture to a boil. Cover and reduce the heat to low. Cook for 40 minutes more or until the vegetables are tender.

3. Stir in the oregano. Serve warm or at room temperature with the crackers.

Makes: 5 cups

1 tablespoon vegetable oil
1 large eggplant, cut in cubes (about 8 cups)
1 Spanish onion, chopped (about 2 cups)
1 large red pepper, chopped (about 1 cup)
2 cloves garlic, minced
1 can (10¾ ounces) Campbell's® Condensed Tomato Soup
1⅓ cups water
1 teaspoon dried oregano leaves, crushed
Pepperidge Farm® Cracker Quartet **or** Cracker Trio Entertaining Collection Cracker Assortment

Fiesta Tortilla Roll-Ups

START TO FINISH: 45 minutes

Prepping: 15 minutes
Refrigerating: 30 minutes

1. Stir the cheese in a 1½-quart bowl until it's smooth. Stir in ½ **cup** of the picante sauce and the green onion.

2. Spread each tortilla with **about ¼ cup** of the cheese mixture. Top each with some spinach, **1 slice** turkey and **2 teaspoons** pimiento. Tightly roll up like a jelly-roll. Place the rolls, seam-side down in a 13×9×2-inch shallow baking dish. Refrigerate for at least 30 minutes or until firm.

3. Cut each roll into 6 slices. Secure each slice with toothpicks. Serve with remaining picante sauce.

Makes: 36 appetizers

1 package (8 ounces) light cream cheese, softened
1 jar (16 ounces) Pace® Picante Sauce
1 medium green onion, chopped (about 2 tablespoons)
6 flour tortillas (8-inch)
1 cup shredded spinach leaves **or romaine lettuce**
6 slices cooked turkey breast (about 6 ounces)
¼ cup chopped pimiento **or** roasted sweet peppers

Game-Winning Drumsticks

START TO FINISH: 5 hours 10 minutes

Prepping: 10 minutes
Marinating: 4 hours
Baking: 1 hour

1. Put the chicken in a single layer in a 15×10-inch disposable aluminum foil bakeware pan.

2. Stir the broth and mustard in a small bowl. Pour the broth mixture over the chicken and turn to coat. Sprinkle the bread crumbs over the chicken. Refrigerate for 4 hours.

3. Bake at 375°F. for 1 hour or until the chicken is cooked through*. Serve immediately or let stand 30 minutes to serve at room temperature, using the pan juices as a dipping sauce.

Makes: About 6 servings

The internal temperature of the chicken should reach 170°F.

15 chicken drumsticks (about 4 pounds)
1¾ cups Swanson® Chicken Broth (Regular, Natural Goodness™ or Certified Organic)
½ cup Dijon-style mustard
⅓ cup Italian-seasoned dry bread crumbs

Appetizers & Snacks

**1 can (10½ ounces)
Campbell's®
Condensed French
Onion Soup
1 package (8 ounces)
cream cheese,
softened
1 cup shredded mozzarella
cheese (4 ounces)
Bread cubes, crackers or
vegetables**

Warm French Onion Dip with Crusty Bread

START TO FINISH: 35 minutes

Prepping: 5 minutes
Baking: 30 minutes

1. Stir the soup and cream cheese in medium bowl until smooth. Stir in the mozzarella cheese. Spread in a 1-quart shallow baking dish.

2. Bake at 375°F. for 30 minutes or until hot.

3. Serve with the bread, crackers or vegetables for dipping.

Makes: 2 cups

Time-Saving Tip: To soften cream cheese, remove from wrapper. On microwavable plate, microwave on HIGH 15 seconds.

Warm Spinach Dip

START TO FINISH: 25 minutes

Prepping: 10 minutes
Cooking: 15 minutes

1. Spray a 2-quart saucepan with cooking spray. Add the onion. Cook and stir until the onion is tender.

2. Stir in the spinach and flour. Gradually stir in the milk. Cook, stirring constantly, until it boils and thickens.

3. Stir in the picante sauce and cheese. Heat until the cheese melts. Season with pepper to taste. Serve with tortilla chips or vegetables for dipping.

Makes: 4 cups

Vegetable cooking spray
½ cup chopped onion
2 packages (10 ounces each) frozen chopped spinach, cooked and well drained
2 tablespoons all-purpose flour
1 cup milk
1 cup Pace® Picante Sauce
1 cup shredded part-skim mozzarella cheese
Ground black pepper

Appetizers & Snacks

Soup's On

Southwestern Chicken & White Bean Soup

1 tablespoon vegetable oil

1 pound skinless, boneless chicken breasts, cut into 1-inch pieces

1¾ cups Swanson® Chicken Broth (Regular, Natural Goodness™ **or** Certified Organic)

1 cup Pace® Chunky Salsa

3 cloves garlic, minced

2 teaspoons ground cumin

1 can (about 16 ounces) small white beans, rinsed and drained

1 cup frozen whole kernel corn

1 large onion, chopped (about 1 cup)

START TO FINISH: 8 to 10 hours 15 minutes

Prepping: 15 minutes
Cooking: 8 to 10 hours

1. Heat the oil in a 10-inch skillet over medium-high heat. Add the chicken and cook until it's well browned on all sides.

2. Mix the broth, salsa, garlic, cumin, beans, corn and onion in a 3½-quart slow cooker. Add the chicken.

3. Cover and cook on LOW for 8 to 10 hours* or until the chicken is cooked through.

Makes: 6 servings

*Or on HIGH for 4 to 5 hours

2 tablespoons vegetable oil
2 large onions, diced
   (about 2 cups)
2 large carrots, diced
   (about 1 cup)
1 tablespoon minced fresh
   ginger
¼ teaspoon ground red
   pepper
6 cups Swanson® Chicken
   Broth (Regular, Natural
   Goodness™ or Certified
   Organic)
2 large sweet potatoes,
   peeled and diced
   (about 3 cups)
1 cup smooth peanut
   butter
⅓ cup sliced green onions
   or chives
⅓ cup chopped peanuts

Soup's On

Spicy Peanut Soup

START TO FINISH: 45 minutes

Prepping: 15 minutes
Cooking: 30 minutes

1. Heat the oil in a 4-quart saucepot over medium heat. Add onions, carrots and ginger and cook until they're tender-crisp. Add the red pepper and cook for 1 minute.

2. Stir in the broth and sweet potatoes and heat to a boil. Cover and reduce the heat to low. Cook for 20 minutes more or until vegetables are tender. Stir in the peanut butter.

3. Place ⅓ of the broth mixture in an electric blender container. Cover and blend until smooth. Pour into a large bowl. Repeat the blending process twice more with the remaining broth mixture. Return all of the puréed mixture to the saucepot and heat through. Season to taste. Sprinkle with the green onions and peanuts.

Makes: 8 servings

Italian Sausage and Spinach Soup

START TO FINISH: 25 minutes

Prepping: 5 minutes
Cooking: 20 minutes

1. Spray a 4-quart saucepot with cooking spray and heat over medium-high heat. Add the sausage and cook until it's well browned.

2. Add the broth, oregano, onion and carrot and heat the mixture to a boil. Cover and reduce the heat to low. Cook for 10 minutes or until the vegetables are tender.

3. Stir in the spinach and cook for 1 minute more.

Makes: 5 servings

Vegetable cooking spray
½ pound sweet Italian pork sausage, cut into ¾-inch slices
4 cups Swanson® Chicken Broth (Regular, Natural Goodness™ **or** Certified Organic)
½ teaspoon dried oregano leaves, crushed
1 medium onion, chopped (about ½ cup)
1 medium carrot, sliced (about ½ cup)
2 cups coarsely chopped fresh spinach leaves

Creamy Beet Soup

START TO FINISH: 30 minutes

Prepping: 10 minutes
Cooking: 20 minutes

2 tablespoons butter
3 medium onions,
chopped (about
1½ cups)
1 potato, peeled and
chopped (about 1 cup)
1 clove garlic, minced
2 cans (14½ ounces **each**)
sliced beets,
undrained
3 cups Swanson® Chicken
Broth (Regular,
Natural Goodness™ **or**
Certified Organic)
1 tablespoon chopped
fresh dill weed **or**
1 teaspoon dried dill
weed, crushed
¼ teaspoon ground black
pepper
Sour cream

1. Heat the butter in a 4-quart saucepot over medium heat. Add the onions and cook until they're tender-crisp. Add the potato and garlic and cook for 1 minute.

2. Drain the liquid from the beets and reserve **1 cup** beet juice. Add the beets and broth to the saucepot and heat to a boil. Cover and reduce the heat to low. Cook for 15 minutes more or until the potato is tender.

3. Place ½ of the broth mixture into an electric blender container. Cover and blend until smooth. Pour into a medium bowl. Repeat the blending process with the remaining broth mixture. Return all of the puréed mixture to the saucepot. Stir in the reserved beet juice, dill and black pepper and heat through. Serve with sour cream.

Makes: 8 servings

Roasted Tomato & Barley Soup

START TO FINISH: 1 hour 15 minutes

Prepping: 10 minutes
Baking: 25 minutes
Cooking: 40 minutes

1. Heat the oven to 425°F. Drain the tomatoes, reserving the juice. Put the tomatoes, onions and garlic in a 17×11-inch roasting pan. Pour the oil over the vegetables and toss to coat. Bake for 25 minutes.

2. Put the roasted vegetables in a 3-quart saucepan. Add the reserved tomato juice, broth, celery and barley and heat to a boil. Cover and reduce the heat to low.

3. Cook for 35 minutes or until the barley is tender. Stir in the parsley.

Makes: 8 servings

1 can (28 ounces) diced tomatoes, undrained
2 large onions, diced (about 2 cups)
2 cloves garlic, minced
2 tablespoons olive oil
4 cups Swanson® Chicken Broth (Regular, Natural Goodness™ **or** Certified Organic)
2 stalks celery, diced (about 1 cup)
½ cup **uncooked** barley
2 tablespoons chopped fresh parsley

1 tablespoon olive **or**
   vegetable oil
1 medium bulb fennel,
   trimmed, cut in half
   and thinly sliced
   (about 2 cups)
1 medium onion, chopped
   (about ½ cup)
1 teaspoon dried thyme
   leaves, crushed
5 cups water
1¾ cups Swanson®
   Vegetable Broth
   (Regular **or** Certified
   Organic)
1 can (10¾ ounces)
   Campbell's® Condensed
   Tomato Soup
1 package (10 ounces)
   frozen baby whole
   carrots, thawed
   (about 1½ cups)
½ pound fresh **or** thawed
   frozen firm white fish
   fillets (cod, haddock **or**
   halibut), cut into 2-inch
   pieces
½ pound fresh large shrimp,
   shelled and deveined
¾ pound mussels (about
   12), well scrubbed
   Freshly ground black
   pepper

Simply Special Seafood Chowder

START TO FINISH: 30 minutes

Prepping: 10 minutes
Cooking: 20 minutes

1. Heat the oil in a 4-quart saucepot over medium heat. Add the fennel, onion and thyme and cook until the vegetables are tender. Stir in the water, broth, soup and carrots and heat to a boil.

2. Stir in the fish. Cook for 2 minutes. Stir in the shrimp and mussels. Cover and reduce the heat to low. Cook for 3 minutes more or until the fish flakes easily when tested with a fork, the shrimp turn pink and the mussels open. Discard any mussels that do not open.

3. Serve the soup with black pepper.

Makes: 6 servings

Creamy Citrus Tomato Soup with Pesto Croutons

START TO FINISH: 15 minutes

Prepping: 10 minutes
Cooking: 5 minutes

1. Stir the soup, milk, cream and lemon juice in a 2-quart saucepan. Heat the soup over medium heat until hot.

2. Spread **1 tablespoon** of the pesto on each toast slice.

3. Divide the soup among 6 serving bowls. Float a pesto crouton on each bowl of soup.

Makes: 6 servings

1 can (10¾ ounces) Campbell's® Condensed Tomato Soup
1 cup milk
½ cup light cream **or** half-and-half
1 tablespoon lemon juice
6 tablespoons prepared pesto
6 slices French **or** Italian bread, ½-inch thick, toasted

Soup's On

½ cup **uncooked** wild rice

½ cup **uncooked** regular long-grain white rice

1 tablespoon vegetable oil

5¼ cups Swanson® Chicken Broth (Regular, Natural Goodness™ **or** Certified Organic)

2 teaspoons dried thyme leaves, crushed

¼ teaspoon crushed red pepper

2 stalks celery, coarsely chopped (about 1 cup)

1 medium onion, chopped (about ½ cup)

1 pound skinless, boneless chicken breasts, cut into cubes

Sour cream (optional)

Chopped green onions (optional)

Soup's On

Slow-Simmered Chicken Rice Soup

START TO FINISH: 7 to 8 hours 30 minutes

Prepping: 15 minutes
Cooking: 7 to 8 hours 15 minutes

1. Mix the wild rice, white rice and oil in a 3½-quart slow cooker. Cover and cook on HIGH for 15 minutes.

2. Stir the broth, thyme, red pepper, celery, onion and chicken to the cooker. Turn the heat to LOW. Cover and cook on LOW for 7 to 8 hours* or until the chicken is cooked through.

3. Serve with the sour cream and green onions, if desired.

Makes: 8 servings

Or on HIGH for 4 to 5 hours

White Bean with Fennel Soup

START TO FINISH: 7 to 8 hours 15 minutes

Prepping: 15 minutes
Cooking: 7 to 8 hours

1. Stir the broth, black pepper, fennel, onion and garlic in a 5½- to 6-quart slow cooker.

2. Cover and cook on LOW for 6 to 7 hours.

3. Add the spinach, tomatoes and undrained beans. Turn the heat to HIGH. Cover and cook for 1 hour more or until the vegetables are tender.

Makes: 6 servings

4 cups Swanson® Vegetable Broth (Regular **or** Certified Organic)
⅛ teaspoon ground black pepper
1 small bulb fennel (about ½ pound), trimmed and sliced (about 2 cups)
1 medium onion, chopped (about ½ cup)
2 cloves garlic, minced
1 package (10 ounces) frozen leaf spinach
1 can (14½ ounces) diced tomatoes
1 can (about 16 ounces) white kidney (cannellini) beans, undrained

Soup's On

1 can (10¾ ounces)
Campbell's® Condensed
Tomato Soup

1 can (10½ ounces)
Campbell's® Condensed
Beef Broth

½ cup Burgundy **or** other
dry red wine **or** water

1 teaspoon dried Italian
seasoning, crushed

½ teaspoon garlic powder

1 can (14½ ounces) diced
Italian-style tomatoes

3 large carrots (about
¾ pound), cut into
1-inch pieces

2 pounds beef for stew, cut
into 1-inch pieces

2 cans (about 16 ounces
each) white kidney
(cannellini) beans,
rinsed and drained

Soup's On

Slow Cooker Tuscan Beef Stew

START TO FINISH: 8 to 9 hours 15 minutes

Prepping: 5 minutes
Cooking: 8 to 9 hours

1. Stir the soup, broth, wine, Italian seasoning, garlic powder, tomatoes, carrots and beef in a 3½-quart slow cooker.

2. Cover and cook on LOW for 8 to 9 hours* or until beef and vegetables are fork-tender.

3. Stir in the beans. Turn the heat to HIGH. Cook for 10 minutes more.

Makes: 8 servings

*Or on HIGH for 4 to 5 hours

Creamy Irish Potato Soup

START TO FINISH: 35 minutes

Prepping: 10 minutes
Cooking: 25 minutes

1. Heat the butter in a 2-quart saucepan over medium-high heat. Add the green onions and celery and cook until the vegetables are tender.

2. Add the broth, water, black pepper and potatoes and heat to a boil. Cover and reduce the heat to low. Cook for 15 minutes more or until the potatoes are tender. Remove from the heat.

3. Place ½ of the broth mixture and ¾ **cup** milk into an electric blender container. Cover and blend until smooth. Pour into a medium bowl. Repeat the blending process with the remaining broth mixture and remaining milk. Return all of the puréed mixture to the saucepan and heat through. Sprinkle with the chives.

Makes: 5 servings

2 tablespoons butter
4 medium green onions, sliced (about ½ cup)
1 stalk celery, sliced (about ½ cup)
1¾ cups Swanson® Chicken Broth (Regular, Natural Goodness™ or Certified Organic)
½ cup water
⅛ teaspoon ground black pepper
3 medium potatoes (about 1 pound), sliced ¼-inch thick
1½ cups milk
Sliced chives

1 jar (16 ounces) Pace®
    Chipotle Chunky Salsa
1 cup water
2 tablespoons chili
    powder
1 large onion, chopped
    (about 1 cup)
2 pounds beef for stew,
    cut into ½-inch pieces
1 can (about 19 ounces)
    red kidney beans,
    rinsed and drained
Shredded Cheddar
    cheese (optional)
Sour cream (optional)

Soup's On

Chipotle Chili

START TO FINISH: 8 to 9 hours 15 minutes

Prepping: 15 minutes
Cooking: 8 to 9 hours

1. Stir the salsa, water, chili powder, onion, beef and beans in a 3½-quart slow cooker.

2. Cover and cook on LOW for 8 to 9 hours* or until the beef is fork-tender.

3. Serve with the cheese and sour cream, if desired.

Makes: 8 servings

Or on HIGH for 4 to 5 hours

Shrimp & Corn Chowder with Sun-Dried Tomatoes

START TO FINISH: 25 minutes

Prepping: 5 minutes
Cooking: 20 minutes

1. Heat the soup, half-and-half, corn and tomatoes in a 2-quart saucepan over medium heat to a boil. Cover and reduce the heat to low. Cook for 10 minutes.

2. Stir in the shrimp and chives and heat through.

3. Season to taste with black pepper.

Makes: 4 servings

Easy Substitution Tip: Substitute skim milk for the half-and-half.

1 can (10¾ ounces)
   Campbell's®
   Condensed Cream
   of Potato Soup
1½ cups half-and-half
2 cups whole kernel corn
2 tablespoons sun-dried
   tomatoes cut in strips
1 cup small **or** medium
   cooked shrimp
2 tablespoons chopped
   fresh chives
   Ground black **or** ground
   red pepper

1 tablespoon olive oil
2 large carrots, coarsely chopped
2 stalks celery, sliced
1 large onion, chopped
3 cloves garlic, minced
2 cans (14 ounces **each**) Swanson® Vegetable Broth
1 can (about 15 ounces) red kidney beans, drained and rinsed
1 can (14½ ounces) diced tomatoes
¼ cup **uncooked** pearl barley
2 cups firmly packed chopped fresh spinach leaves
Ground black pepper

Hearty Bean & Barley Soup

START TO FINISH: 55 minutes

Prepping: 15 minutes
Cooking: 40 minutes

1. Heat the oil in a 4-quart saucepot over medium-high heat. Add the carrots, celery, onion and garlic. Cook and stir until the vegetables are tender.

2. Stir in the broth, beans, tomatoes and barley. Heat to a boil. Reduce the heat to low. Cover and cook for 30 minutes or until the barley is done.

3. Stir in the spinach and season to taste with black pepper. Heat through.

Makes: 6 servings

Spaghetti Soup

START TO FINISH: 45 minutes

Prepping: 15 minutes
Cooking: 30 minutes

1. Heat **1 tablespoon** oil in a saucepot over medium-high heat. Add the chicken and cook until it's browned, stirring often. Remove the chicken.

2. Stir in the remaining oil and heat over medium heat. Add the onion and cook for 1 minute. Add the carrots and cook for 1 minute. Add the celery and garlic and cook for 1 minute.

3. Stir in the broth, soup and water. Heat to a boil. Stir in the pasta. Cook for 10 minutes or until pasta is tender. Add the chicken and parsley, if desired, and heat through.

Makes: 4 servings

2 tablespoons vegetable oil
½ pound skinless, boneless chicken breasts, cut into cubes
1 medium onion, chopped (about ½ cup)
1 large carrot, chopped (about ½ cup)
1 stalk celery, finely chopped (about ⅓ cup)
2 cloves garlic, minced
4 cups Swanson® Chicken Broth (Regular, Natural Goodness™ **or** Certified Organic)
1 can (10¾ ounces) Campbell's® Condensed Tomato Soup
1 cup water
3 ounces spaghetti, broken into 1-inch pieces
2 tablespoons chopped fresh parsley (optional)

30-Minute Dishes

Southwest Salsa Chicken with Fresh Greens

1 tablespoon chili powder
1 teaspoon ground cumin
1½ pounds skinless, boneless chicken breast halves, cut into strips
1 tablespoon olive oil
1 cup Pace® Chunky Salsa
¼ cup water
1 bag (about 7 ounces) mixed salad greens (6 cups)

START TO FINISH: 20 minutes

Prepping: 10 minutes
Cooking: 10 minutes

1. Mix the chili powder and cumin in a shallow dish. Coat the chicken with the seasonings.

2. Heat the oil in a heavy 12-inch skillet over high heat. Add the chicken and cook until the chicken is blackened and cooked through*, stirring often. Remove the chicken and set aside.

3. Stir in the salsa and water. Cook and stir over medium heat until mixture is hot and bubbling. Divide the salad greens among 6 plates. Top each with chicken and salsa.

Makes: 6 servings

The internal temperature of the chicken should reach 160°F.

2 slices Pepperidge Farm®
    Sandwich White
    Bread, torn into pieces
⅓ cup shredded Parmesan
    cheese
1 clove garlic
½ teaspoon dried thyme
    leaves, crushed
⅛ teaspoon ground black
    pepper
2 tablespoons olive oil
8 fresh tilapia fish fillets
    (3 to 4 ounces **each**)
1 egg, beaten

Italian Fish Fillets

START TO FINISH: 20 minutes

Prepping: 10 minutes
Baking: 10 minutes

1. Place the bread, cheese, garlic, thyme and black pepper in an electric blender container. Cover and blend until fine crumbs form. Slowly add the olive oil and blend until moistened.

2. Put the fish fillets in a 17×11-inch roasting pan. Brush with the egg. Divide the bread crumb mixture evenly over the fillets.

3. Bake at 400°F. for 10 minutes or until the fish flakes easily when tested with a fork and the crumb topping is golden.

Makes: 8 servings

Easy Substitution Tip: Substitute about 2 pounds firm white fish fillets such as cod, haddock or halibut for the tilapia fillets.

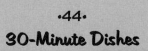

Chicken & Black Bean Quesadillas

START TO FINISH: 20 minutes

Prepping: 5 minutes
Cooking/Baking: 15 minutes

1. Stir the soup, salsa, beans and chicken in a 1½-quart saucepan. Cook and stir over medium heat until hot.

2. Put the tortillas on 2 baking sheets. Top half of each tortilla with **about ⅓ cup** of the soup mixture, spreading to within ½ inch of the edge. Moisten the edge of each tortilla with water. Fold over and press the edges together to seal.

3. Bake at 425°F. for 5 minutes or until the filling is hot. Serve with *Fiesta Rice*.

Makes: 10 quesadillas

Fiesta Rice: Heat **1 can** (10½ ounces) Campbell's® Condensed Chicken Broth, ½ **cup** water and ½ **cup** Pace® Chunky Salsa in a 1½-quart saucepan to a boil. Stir in **2 cups uncooked** instant white rice. Cover and remove from the heat. Let stand for 5 minutes, and then fluff the rice with a fork.

1 can (10¾ ounces) Campbell's® Condensed Cheddar Cheese Soup
½ cup Pace® Chunky Salsa **or** Picante Sauce
1 cup canned black beans, rinsed and drained
2 cans (4.5 ounces **each**) Swanson® Premium Chunk Chicken Breast, drained
10 flour tortillas (8-inch)

Grilled Fish Steaks with Chunky Tomato Sauce

START TO FINISH: 25 minutes

Prepping: 5 minutes
Cooking/Grilling: 20 minutes

1. Spray a 1½-quart saucepan with cooking spray. Heat over medium heat for 1 minute. Add the celery, green pepper, onion, thyme and garlic powder. Cook until the vegetables are tender.

2. Add the soup, lemon juice and hot pepper sauce and heat to a boil. Cover and reduce the heat to low. Cook for 5 minutes or until hot.

3. Lightly oil the grill rack and heat the grill to medium. Grill the fish for 10 minutes or until the fish flakes easily when tested with a fork, turning the fish over halfway through cooking. Serve the sauce over the fish.

Makes: 6 servings

Vegetable cooking spray
1 stalk celery, chopped (about ½ cup)
1 small green pepper, chopped (about ½ cup)
1 medium onion, chopped (about ½ cup)
½ teaspoon dried thyme leaves, crushed
¼ teaspoon garlic powder **or** 2 cloves garlic, minced
1 can (10¾ ounces) Campbell's® Healthy Request® Condensed Tomato Soup
2 tablespoons lemon juice
⅛ teaspoon hot pepper sauce (optional)
6 fresh halibut steaks, 1-inch thick (about 2¼ pounds)

Beef 'n' Bean Burritos

START TO FINISH: 15 minutes

Prepping: 5 minutes
Cooking/Baking: 10 minutes

1. Cook the beef and onion in a 10-inch skillet over medium-high heat until the beef is well browned, stirring frequently to break up meat. Pour off any fat.

2. Stir in the soup and water. Cook until the mixture is hot and bubbling.

3. Spoon **about ⅓ cup** of the beef mixture down the center of each tortilla. Top with cheese, salsa and sour cream. Fold the sides of the tortilla over the filling and then fold up the ends to enclose the filling.

Makes: 8 burritos

1 pound ground beef
1 small onion, chopped (about ¼ cup)
1 can (11.25 ounces) Campbell's® Condensed Fiesta Chili Beef Soup
¼ cup water
8 flour tortillas (8-inch), warmed
  Shredded Cheddar cheese
  Pace® Chunky Salsa
  Sour cream

1 can (10¾ ounces)
    Campbell's®
    Condensed Creamy
    Chicken Verde Soup
½ teaspoon garlic powder
1½ cups chopped cooked
    chicken
⅔ cup shredded Cheddar
    or Monterey Jack
    cheese
8 corn tortillas (6-inch),
    warmed
¼ cup milk

Creamy Enchiladas Verde

START TO FINISH: 30 minutes

Prepping: 10 minutes
Baking: 20 minutes

1. Mix ½ **can** of the soup, garlic powder, chicken and ⅓ **cup** cheese in a medium bowl.

2. Spoon **about ⅓ cup** of the chicken mixture down the center of each tortilla. Roll up the tortillas and place them seam-side down in 2-quart shallow baking dish. Mix the remaining soup and milk in a small bowl and pour over the filled tortillas. Top with the remaining cheese.

3. Bake at 375°F. for 20 minutes or until the enchiladas are hot and bubbly.

Makes: 4 servings

30-Minute Dishes

Quick Ranchero Chili

START TO FINISH: 25 minutes

Prepping: 5 minutes
Cooking: 20 minutes

1. Cook the beef, onion and chili powder in a 10-inch skillet over medium-high heat until the beef is well browned, stirring frequently to break up the meat. Pour off any fat.

2. Stir in the soup, water and beans and heat to a boil.

3. Cover and reduce the heat to low. Cook for 10 minutes. Top with the cheese.

Makes: 4 servings

1 pound ground beef
1 medium onion, chopped
  (about ½ cup)
2 tablespoons chili
  powder
1 can (10¾ ounces)
  Campbell's®
  Condensed Creamy
  Ranchero Tomato
  Soup
½ cup water
1 can (about 15 ounces)
  small red beans **or red
  kidney beans, rinsed
  and drained**
  Shredded Cheddar
  cheese

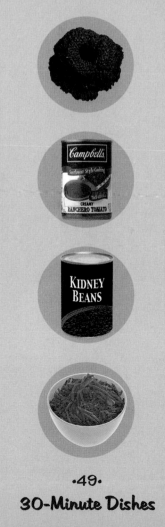

¾ cup Pace® Picante Sauce
½ cup plain yogurt
1 teaspoon lime juice
¼ teaspoon garlic powder **or 2 cloves garlic,** minced
1 pound boneless pork chops, ¾-inch thick
6 pita breads (6-inch), warmed
1 cup shredded lettuce
1 medium green onion, sliced (about 2 tablespoons)

Grilled Pork in Pitas

START TO FINISH: 25 minutes

Prepping: 10 minutes
Grilling: 15 minutes

1. Mix **3 tablespoons** picante sauce, yogurt and lime juice. Refrigerate until ready to serve. Mix the remaining picante sauce and garlic powder in a small bowl.

2. Lightly oil the grill rack and heat the grill to medium-high. Grill the pork chops for 15 minutes or until chops are cooked through but slightly pink in center*, turning and brushing them often with the picante sauce mixture while they're grilling. Discard remaining picante sauce mixture.

3. Slice the pork into thin strips. Spoon the pork down the center of the pita. Top with the yogurt mixture, lettuce and green onion. Fold pita around filling.

Makes: 6 sandwiches

The internal temperature of the pork should reach 160°F.

Time-Saving Tip: To warm the pita breads, wrap them in a plain paper towel. Microwave on HIGH for 1 minute or until warm.

Tomato-Basil Chicken

START TO FINISH: 25 minutes

Prepping: 10 minutes
Cooking: 15 minutes

1. Heat the oil in a 10-inch skillet over medium-high heat. Add the chicken and cook for 10 minutes or until it's well browned on both sides. Remove the chicken and set aside.

2. Stir in the soup, milk, cheese, basil and garlic powder. Heat to a boil. Return the chicken to the skillet and reduce the heat to low. Cover and cook for 5 minutes or until the chicken is cooked through*.

3. Serve with the pasta.

Makes: 6 servings

*The internal temperature of the chicken should reach 160°F.

1 tablespoon vegetable oil
1½ pounds skinless, boneless chicken breast halves (about 4 to 6)
1 can (10¾ ounces) Campbell's® Condensed Tomato Soup
½ cup milk
2 tablespoons grated Parmesan cheese
½ teaspoon dried basil leaves, crushed
¼ teaspoon garlic powder or 2 cloves garlic, minced
3 cups medium tube-shaped pasta (ziti), cooked and drained

1 pound ground beef
1 can (10½ ounces) Campbell's® Condensed French Onion Soup
4 slices cheese
4 round hard rolls, split

French Onion Burgers

START TO FINISH: 25 minutes

Prepping: 5 minutes
Cooking: 20 minutes

1. Shape the beef into 4 (½-inch) thick burgers.

2. Heat a 10-inch skillet over medium-high heat. Add the burgers and cook until they're well browned on both sides. Remove the burgers and set aside. Pour off any fat.

3. Stir in the soup into the skillet. Heat to a boil. Return the burgers to the skillet and reduce the heat to low. Cover and cook for 5 minutes or until the burgers are cooked through*. Top with cheese and continue cooking until the cheese melts. Serve burgers in rolls with soup mixture for dipping.

Makes: 4 burgers

The internal temperature of the burgers should reach 160°F.

Quick Chicken Parmesan

START TO FINISH: 15 minutes

Prepping: 5 minutes
Baking: 10 minutes

1. Spread **1 cup** of the pasta sauce in a 12×8×2-inch shallow baking dish.

2. Place the chicken cutlets over the sauce. Spoon ¼ **cup** of the remaining pasta sauce down the center of each cutlet. Top each with **1 slice** ham and ¼ **cup** mozzarella cheese. Sprinkle with the Parmesan cheese.

3. Bake at 425°F. for 10 minutes or until the cheese melts and the sauce is hot and bubbly.

Makes: 4 servings

2 cups Prego® Traditional
    Pasta Sauce
4 fully cooked breaded
    chicken cutlets
4 thin slices cooked ham
1 cup shredded mozzarella
    cheese (4 ounces)
2 tablespoons grated
    Parmesan cheese

1 tablespoon vegetable oil
4 bone-in pork chops,
    ½-inch thick (about
    1 pound)
1 can (10¾ ounces)
    Campbell's®
    Condensed Cream of
    Celery Soup (Regular
    or 98% Fat Free)
½ cup apple juice **or** water
2 tablespoons spicy-brown
    mustard
1 tablespoon honey
    Generous dash ground
    black pepper
    Hot cooked medium egg
    noodles

Autumn Pork Chops

START TO FINISH: 25 minutes

Prepping: 5 minutes
Cooking: 20 minutes

1. Heat the oil in a 10-inch skillet over medium-high heat. Add the pork chops and cook until the chops are well browned on both sides. Remove the pork chops and set them aside.

2. Stir in the soup, apple juice, mustard, honey and black pepper. Heat to a boil. Return the pork chops to the skillet and reduce the heat to low. Cover and cook for 5 minutes or until chops are cooked through but slightly pink in the center*.

3. Serve with the noodles.

Makes: 4 servings

The internal temperature of the pork should reach 160°F.

30-Minute Dishes

Cranberry Chicken

START TO FINISH: 25 minutes

Prepping: 5 minutes
Cooking: 20 minutes

1. Heat the oil in a 10-inch skillet over medium-high heat. Add the chicken and cook for 10 minutes or until it's well browned on both sides. Remove the chicken and set aside.

2. Stir in the soup, cranberry juice, orange juice, cranberries, sage and black pepper. Heat to a boil. Return the chicken to the skillet and reduce the heat to low. Cover and cook for 5 minutes or until the chicken is cooked through*.

3. Serve the chicken with the rice.

Makes: 6 servings

The internal temperature of the chicken should reach 160°F.

1 tablespoon vegetable oil
1½ pounds skinless, boneless
    chicken breast halves
    (about 4 to 6)
1 can (10¾ ounces)
    Campbell's® Condensed
    Cream of Mushroom
    Soup (Regular **or**
    98% Fat Free)
¼ cup cranberry juice
¼ cup orange juice
1 tablespoon dried
    cranberries
1 tablespoon chopped
    fresh sage leaves **or**
    1 teaspoon dried sage
    leaves, crushed
⅛ teaspoon ground black
    pepper
    Hot cooked rice

2 tablespoons vegetable oil
2 tablespoons lemon juice
1 tablespoon
    Worcestershire sauce
1 teaspoon Cajun
    seasoning
1 pound **uncooked** large
    shrimp, shelled and
    deveined
1 medium onion, chopped
    (about ½ cup)
2 cloves garlic, minced
1 can (10¾ ounces)
    Campbell's®
    Condensed Cream of
    Chicken with Herbs
    Soup
½ cup milk
1 teaspoon paprika
    Cornbread **or** biscuits

New Orleans Shrimp Toss

START TO FINISH: 25 minutes

Prepping: 10 minutes
Cooking: 15 minutes

1. Mix **1 tablespoon** oil, lemon juice, Worcestershire and Cajun seasoning in a medium bowl. Add the shrimp and toss lightly to coat.

2. Heat the remaining oil in a 10-inch skillet over medium-high heat. Add the onion and garlic. Cook and stir until the onion is tender.

3. Stir in the soup, milk and paprika. Heat to a boil. Add the shrimp mixture to the skillet and reduce the heat to low. Cover and cook for 5 minutes or until the shrimp turn pink. Serve with the cornbread.

Makes: 4 servings

Skillet Cheesy Chicken and Rice

START TO FINISH: 25 minutes

Prepping: 5 minutes
Cooking: 20 minutes

1. Heat the oil in a 10-inch skillet over medium-high heat. Add the chicken and cook for 10 minutes or until it's well browned on both sides. Remove the chicken and set aside.

2. Stir in the soup, water, paprika and black pepper. Heat to a boil.

3. Stir in the broccoli and rice. Return the chicken to the skillet and reduce the heat to low. Sprinkle the chicken with additional paprika and black pepper. Top with the cheese. Cover and cook for 5 minutes or until chicken is cooked through* and the rice is tender.

Makes: 6 servings

The internal temperature of the chicken should reach 160°F.

1 tablespoon vegetable oil
1½ pounds skinless, boneless chicken breast halves (about 4 to 6)
1 can (10¾ ounces) Campbell's® Condensed Cream of Chicken Soup (Regular or 98% Fat Free)
1½ cups water
¼ teaspoon paprika
¼ teaspoon ground black pepper
2 cups fresh or frozen broccoli flowerets
1½ cups uncooked instant white rice
½ cup shredded Cheddar cheese

2 tablespoons olive **or** vegetable oil

1½ pounds skinless, boneless chicken breasts, cut into strips

4 cups sliced mushrooms (about 12 ounces)

1 tablespoon minced garlic

1 tablespoon chopped fresh rosemary leaves **or** 1 teaspoon dried rosemary leaves, crushed

1 can (14½ ounces) Campbell's® Chicken Gravy

1 package (16 ounces) linguine or spaghetti, cooked and drained

Shredded Parmesan cheese

Rosemary Chicken & Mushroom Pasta

START TO FINISH: 30 minutes

Prepping: 10 minutes
Cooking: 20 minutes

1. Heat the oil in a 12-inch skillet over medium-high heat. Add the chicken and mushrooms and cook in 2 batches or until it's well browned, stirring often. Remove the chicken and mushrooms and set them aside.

2. Reduce the heat to low. Stir the garlic and rosemary into the skillet and cook for 1 minute. Stir the gravy into the skillet. Heat to a boil.

3. Return the chicken and mushrooms to the skillet. Cover and cook for 5 minutes or until the chicken is cooked through*. Place the pasta in a 3-quart serving bowl. Pour the chicken mixture over the pasta. Toss to coat. Serve with the cheese.

Makes: 6 servings

The internal temperature of the chicken should reach 160°F.

Poached Halibut with Pineapple Salsa

START TO FINISH: 25 minutes

Prepping: 10 minutes
Cooking: 15 minutes

1. Drain the pineapple and reserve ⅔ **cup** juice.

2. Mix the pineapple chunks, cucumber, red pepper, red onion, vinegar and hot pepper sauce, if desired, in a medium bowl and set aside.

3. Heat the broth, wine and reserved pineapple juice in a 12-inch skillet over high heat to a boil. Add the fish and reduce the heat to low. Cover and cook for 10 minutes or until the fish flakes easily when tested with a fork. Serve the fish with the pineapple salsa.

Makes: 4 servings

1 can (15¼ ounces) pineapple chunks in juice, undrained
1 seedless cucumber, peeled and diced (about 1⅔ cups)
1 medium red pepper, chopped (about ¾ cup)
2 tablespoons chopped red onion
1 teaspoon white wine vinegar
1 teaspoon hot pepper sauce (optional)
1¾ cups Swanson® Chicken Broth (Regular, Natural Goodness™ **or** Certified Organic)
¼ cup white wine
4 fresh halibut fillets (about 1½ pounds)

30-Minute Dishes

1 pound ground beef
1 can (10¾ ounces)
   Campbell's®
   Condensed Tomato
   Soup
¾ cup Pace® Picante Sauce
1 teaspoon ground cumin
1 cup frozen whole kernel
   corn
1 can (11 ounces)
   Campbell's®
   Condensed Fiesta
   Nacho Cheese Soup
1 cup milk
2 tablespoons butter
1⅓ cups instant mashed
   potato flakes **or** buds

Fast Fiesta Shepherd's Pie

START TO FINISH: 20 minutes

Prepping: 5 minutes
Cooking: 15 minutes

1. Cook the beef in a 10-inch skillet over medium-high heat until it's well browned, stirring frequently to break up meat. Pour off any fat.

2. Stir in the tomato soup, picante sauce, cumin and corn and heat to a boil. Reduce the heat to low and cook for 5 minutes, stirring occasionally.

3. Heat the cheese soup, milk and butter in 2-quart saucepan over medium-high heat to a boil. Remove from the heat. Stir in the potato flakes. Let stand for 30 seconds. Mix with a fork until it's evenly moistened. Drop the potato mixture by large spoonfuls onto the beef mixture.

Makes: 4 servings

Balsamic Glazed Salmon

START TO FINISH: 25 minutes

Prepping: 5 minutes
Baking/Cooking: 20 minutes

1. Place the salmon in a 12×8×2-inch shallow baking dish. Sprinkle with black pepper and drizzle with oil. Bake at 350°F. for 15 minutes or until the fish flakes easily when tested with a fork.

2. Stir the cornstarch, broth, vinegar, orange juice, brown sugar and orange peel in a 2-quart saucepan over high heat. Heat the mixture to a boil. Continue to cook until the mixture thickens, stirring constantly.

3. Place the salmon on a serving platter and serve with the sauce.

Makes: 8 servings

8 fresh salmon fillets,
   ¾-inch thick (about
   1½ pounds)
   Freshly ground black
   pepper
3 tablespoons olive oil
4½ teaspoons cornstarch
1¾ cups Swanson® Chicken
   Broth (Regular, Natural
   Goodness™ **or**
   Certified Organic)
3 tablespoons balsamic
   vinegar
1 tablespoon orange juice
1 tablespoon brown sugar
1 teaspoon grated orange
   peel

2 tablespoons olive oil
2 large onions, thinly
   sliced (about 2 cups)
2 pounds boneless beef
   sirloin, strip or rib
   steaks, cut into
   8 pieces
1 jar (16 ounces) Pace®
   Chunky Salsa

Grilled Beef Steak with Sautéed Onions

START TO FINISH: 30 minutes

Prepping: 5 minutes
Cooking/Grilling: 25 minutes

1. Heat **1 tablespoon** oil in a 12-inch skillet over medium heat. Add the onions and cook until they're tender. Remove the onions from the skillet and keep warm.

2. Heat the remaining oil in the skillet. Add the steak pieces and cook until they're well browned on both sides.

3. Add the salsa and return the onions to the skillet. Cook for 3 minutes for medium-rare* or until desired doneness.

Makes: 8 servings

The internal temperature of the steak should reach 145°F.

Monterey Chicken Fajitas

START TO FINISH: 20 minutes

Prepping: 5 minutes
Cooking: 15 minutes

1. Heat the oil in a 10-inch skillet over medium-high heat. Add the chicken and cook and stir until it's well browned.

2. Reduce the heat to medium. Add the pepper and onion. Cook and stir until the vegetables are tender-crisp. Stir in the soup and salsa. Cook until the chicken is cooked through*.

3. Spoon **about ½ cup** of the chicken mixture down the center of each tortilla. Top with the cheese and additional salsa. Fold the tortilla around the filling.

Makes: 8 fajitas

The internal temperature of the chicken should reach 160°F.

2 tablespoons vegetable oil
1 pound skinless, boneless chicken breasts, cut into strips
1 medium green pepper, cut into 2-inch-long strips (about 1½ cups)
1 medium onion, sliced (about ½ cup)
1 can (10¾ ounces) Campbell's® Condensed Cream of Mushroom Soup (Regular **or** 98% Fat Free)
½ cup Pace® Chunky Salsa
8 flour tortillas (8-inch), warmed
1 cup shredded Monterey Jack cheese (4 ounces)

1 can (10¾ ounces)
   Campbell's Condensed
   Tomato Soup
2 tablespoons packed
   brown sugar
2 tablespoons lemon juice
2 tablespoons vegetable
   oil
1 tablespoon
   Worcestershire sauce
1 teaspoon garlic powder
¼ teaspoon dried thyme
   leaves, crushed
1½ pounds boneless beef
   sirloin steak, ¾-inch
   thick

Tangy Grilled Beef

START TO FINISH: 30 minutes

Prepping: 5 minutes
Grilling/Cooking: 15 minutes
Standing: 10 minutes

1. Stir the soup, sugar, lemon juice, oil, Worcestershire, garlic powder and thyme in a medium bowl.

2. Lightly oil the grill rack and heat the grill to medium. Grill the steak for 10 minutes for medium-rare* or until desired doneness, turning the steak over halfway through cooking and brushing it often with some of the soup mixture. Let it stand for 10 minutes before slicing.

3. Pour the remaining soup mixture into a 1-quart saucepan. Heat over medium-high heat to a boil. Serve the sauce with the steak.

Makes: 6 servings

The internal temperature of the steak should reach 145°F.

Chicken Scampi

START TO FINISH: 25 minutes

Prepping: 5 minutes
Cooking: 20 minutes

1. Heat the butter in a 10-inch skillet over medium-high heat. Add the chicken and cook for 10 minutes or until it's well browned on both sides. Remove the chicken and set aside.

2. Stir in the soup, water, lemon juice and garlic into the skillet. Heat to a boil. Return the chicken to the skillet and reduce the heat to low. Cover and cook for 5 minutes or until chicken is cooked through*.

3. Serve the chicken with the pasta.

Makes: 4 servings

The internal temperature of the chicken should reach 160°F.

2 tablespoons butter
1½ pounds skinless, boneless chicken breast halves (about 4 to 6)
1 can (10¾ ounces) Campbell's® Condensed Cream of Chicken Soup (Regular or 98% Fat Free)
¼ cup water
2 teaspoons lemon juice
2 cloves garlic, minced or ½ teaspoon garlic powder
Hot cooked pasta

Family Favorites

Ranchero Oven-Fried Chicken

START TO FINISH: 1 hour

Prepping: 10 minutes
Baking: 50 minutes

2 cups Pepperidge Farm®
    Herb Seasoned **or**
    Corn Bread Stuffing,
    crushed
½ cup all-purpose flour
1 can (10¾ ounces)
    Campbell's®
    Condensed Creamy
    Ranchero Tomato
    Soup
1 tablespoon water
4 pounds chicken parts
    (breasts, thighs,
    drumsticks)

1. Put the crushed stuffing and flour on 2 separate plates.

2. Stir the soup and water in a shallow dish. Lightly coat the chicken with the flour. Dip the chicken into the soup mixture, then coat with the stuffing crumbs.

3. Put the chicken on a baking sheet. Bake at 400°F. for 50 minutes or until the chicken is cooked through*. Serve the chicken warm or at room temperature.

*The internal temperature of the chicken parts should reach 170°F.

Makes: 8 servings

Cooking for a Crowd: Recipe may be doubled.

Make Ahead: Prepare the chicken as directed and cool for 30 minutes. Cover and refrigerate the chicken for up to 24 hours. When ready to serve, place the chicken on a baking sheet and bake at 350°F. for 30 minutes or until hot.

Beef Stroganoff

START TO FINISH: 20 minutes

Prepping: 10 minutes
Cooking: 10 minutes

1. Sprinkle the beef with the black pepper.

2. Heat the oil in a 10-inch skillet over medium-high heat. Add the beef and cook until it's well browned on all sides, stirring often. Remove the beef with a slotted spoon and set it aside.

3. Reduce the heat to medium. Add the onion. Cook and stir until the onion is tender. Stir in the soup, water, sherry, if desired, and tomato paste. Heat to a boil. Return the beef to the skillet and heat through. Remove from the heat. Stir in the yogurt. Serve over the noodles and sprinkle with the parsley.

Makes: 4 servings

1 pound boneless beef sirloin **or** top round steak, ¾-inch thick, cut into 2-inch pieces
Cracked black pepper
1 tablespoon vegetable oil
1 medium onion, finely chopped (about ½ cup)
1 can (10¾ ounces) Campbell's® Condensed Cream of Mushroom Soup (Regular **or** 98% Fat Free)
½ cup water
¼ cup dry sherry (optional)
1 tablespoon tomato paste
¼ cup plain yogurt
Hot cooked medium egg noodles
Chopped fresh parsley

Autumn Brisket

START TO FINISH: 8 to 9 hours 20 minutes

Prepping: 20 minutes
Cooking: 8 to 9 hours

1. Season brisket if desired.

2. Place the brisket in a 6-quart slow cooker. Top with the cabbage, sweet potato, onion and apple. Stir the soup, water and caraway, if desired, in a medium bowl. Pour the soup mixture over the brisket and vegetable mixture.

3. Cover and cook on for LOW 8 to 9 hours* or until the brisket is fork-tender.

Makes: 8 servings

*Or on HIGH for 4 to 5 hours

3-pound boneless beef brisket

1 small head cabbage (about 1 pound), cut into 8 wedges

1 large sweet potato (about ¾ pound), peeled and cut into 1-inch pieces

1 large onion, cut into 8 wedges

1 medium Granny Smith apple, cored and cut into 8 wedges

2 cans (10¾ ounces **each**) Campbell's® Condensed Cream of Celery Soup (Regular **or** 98% Fat Free)

1 cup water

2 teaspoons caraway seed (optional)

Family Favorites

3 tablespoons butter
1½ pounds skinless,
    boneless chicken
    breast halves
    (about 4 to 6)
1 box (6 ounces)
    Pepperidge Farm® One
    Step Chicken Flavored
    Stuffing Mix
1¼ cups water
1 can (10¾ ounces)
    Campbell's®
    Condensed Cream of
    Chicken Soup (Regular
    or 98% Fat Free)
½ cup milk
½ cup shredded Cheddar
    cheese

Chicken & Stuffing Skillet

START TO FINISH: 25 minutes

Prepping: 5 minutes
Cooking: 20 minutes

1. Heat **1 tablespoon** butter in a 10-inch skillet over medium-high heat. Add the chicken and cook for 12 to 15 minutes or until the chicken is cooked through*. Remove the chicken and set it aside.

2. Prepare the stuffing in the skillet using the water and the remaining butter according to the package directions **except** let it stand for 2 minutes.

3. Return the chicken to the skillet and reduce the heat to medium. Stir the soup and milk in a small bowl and pour it over the chicken. Sprinkle with the cheese. Cover and cook until the mixture is hot and bubbling.

Makes: 6 servings

The internal temperature of the chicken should reach 160°F.

Family Favorites

Easy Chicken & Pasta Salad

START TO FINISH: 50 minutes

Prepping: 20 minutes
Refrigerating: 30 minutes

1. Mix the pasta, chicken, zucchini, mushrooms and tomatoes in a 3-quart bowl.

2. Pour the dressing over the pasta mixture, tossing until well coated. Cover and refrigerate the salad for 30 minutes.

3. Stir the salad before serving.

Makes: 8 (1 cup) servings

Cooking for a Crowd: Recipe may be doubled.

Make Ahead: Prepare the salad as directed. Cover and refrigerate overnight. Stir the salad before serving.

2 cups corkscrew pasta, cooked and drained
2 cans (4½ ounces each) Swanson® Premium Chunk Chicken Breast, drained
1 large zucchini, cut in half lengthwise and sliced (about 1½ cups)
1 cup sliced mushrooms
1 cup cherry tomatoes, cut into quarters
¾ cup prepared creamy fat free Italian herb salad dressing

Vegetable cooking spray
1 package (about 4 ounces) butter-flavored instant mashed potatoes flakes (about 1¼ cups)
½ cup shredded Cheddar cheese
2 teaspoons dried oregano leaves, crushed
⅓ cup mayonnaise
3 pounds skinless, boneless chicken breast halves (about 8 to 10)

Potato Crusted Chicken

START TO FINISH: 35 minutes

Prepping: 10 minutes
Baking: 25 minutes

1. Heat the oven to 400°F. Spray a baking sheet with the cooking spray.

2. Mix the potatoes, cheese and oregano in a shallow bowl. Brush the mayonnaise on both sides of the chicken. Dip the chicken into the potato mixture to coat well on both sides. Place the chicken on the prepared pan.

3. Bake for 25 minutes or until chicken is cooked through* and coating is golden brown.

Makes: 12 servings

The internal temperature of the chicken should reach 160°F.

Family Favorites

Creamy Chicken Bake

START TO FINISH: 40 minutes

Prepping: 10 minutes
Baking: 30 minutes

1. Place the chicken in a 13×9×2-inch shallow baking dish. Mix the soup, milk, garlic powder and mushrooms in a medium bowl and pour over the chicken.

2. Mix the cheese and bread crumbs with the butter in a small bowl and sprinkle over the soup mixture.

3. Bake at 400°F. for 30 minutes or until chicken is cooked through*. Place the chicken on a serving plate. Stir the sauce and serve with the chicken.

Makes: 6 servings

The internal temperature of the chicken should reach 160°F.

1½ **pounds skinless, boneless chicken breast halves (about 4 to 6)**
1 **can (10¾ ounces) Campbell's® Condensed Cream of Broccoli Soup (Regular or 98% Fat Free)**
⅓ **cup milk**
½ **teaspoon garlic powder**
1 **jar (4½ ounces) sliced mushrooms, drained**
¼ **cup grated Parmesan cheese**
¼ **cup dry bread crumbs**
2 **tablespoons butter, melted**

2 tablespoons cornstarch
1¾ cups Swanson® Chicken Broth (Regular, Natural Goodness™ **or** Certified Organic)
2 tablespoons soy sauce
½ teaspoon ground ginger
½ teaspoon sesame oil (optional)
2 tablespoons vegetable **or** canola oil
1 pound skinless, boneless chicken breasts, cut into strips
2 cups broccoli flowerets
2 small red peppers, cut into 2-inch-long strips (about 2 cups)
2 cloves garlic, minced
½ cup salted peanuts
Hot cooked rice

Family Favorites

Asian Chicken & Rice

START TO FINISH: 30 minutes

Prepping: 15 minutes
Cooking: 15 minutes

1. Stir the cornstarch, broth, soy, ginger and sesame oil in a medium bowl. Set the mixture aside.

2. Heat **1 tablespoon** oil in a 12-inch skillet over medium-high heat. Add the chicken and stir-fry until it's browned. Remove the chicken with a slotted spoon and set it aside.

3. Reduce the heat to medium and add the remaining oil. Add the broccoli, pepper and garlic. Stir-fry until the vegetables are tender-crisp. Stir the cornstarch mixture and stir it into the skillet. Cook and stir until the mixture boils and thickens. Return the chicken to the skillet and add the peanuts and cook until the mixture is hot and bubbling. Serve over the rice.

Makes: 4 servings

Cranberry Dijon Pork Chops

START TO FINISH: 55 minutes

Prepping: 10 minutes
Cooking/Baking: 45 minutes

1. Heat the oil in a 10-inch oven-safe skillet over medium-high heat. Add the pork chops and cook until the chops are well browned on both sides. Remove the pork chops and set them aside.

2. Stir in the soup, cranberry juice, mustard and thyme. Heat to a boil. Return the pork chops to the skillet and cover.

3. Bake at 350°F. for 45 minutes or until chops are cooked through but slightly pink in center*. Place the pork chops on a serving plate. Stir the cranberries into the skillet. Serve the sauce with the pork and noodles.

Makes: 4 servings

The internal temperature of the pork should reach 160°F.

1 tablespoon olive oil
4 boneless pork chops, 1-inch thick (about 1¼ pounds)
1 can (10¾ ounces) Campbell's® Condensed Cream of Celery Soup (Regular or 98% Fat Free)
½ cup cranberry juice
2 tablespoons Dijon-style mustard
¼ teaspoon dried thyme leaves, crushed
¼ cup dried cranberries **or** cherries
Hot cooked noodles

2 tablespoons olive oil

1½ pounds boneless beef sirloin **or** top round steak, ¾-inch thick, cut into ½-inch pieces

1 medium onion, chopped (about ½ cup)

2 cloves garlic, minced

3 cups Pace® Chunky Salsa, any variety

½ cup water

1 tablespoon chili powder

1 teaspoon ground cumin

1 can (about 15 ounces) red kidney beans, rinsed and drained

¼ cup chopped fresh cilantro leaves

Chili Toppings (optional) chopped tomatoes, chopped onions **or** shredded cheese

Family Favorites

Smokin' Texas Chili

START TO FINISH: 2 hours

Prepping: 15 minutes
Cooking: 1 hour 45 minutes

1. Heat **1 tablespoon** oil in a 4-quart saucepot over medium-high heat. Add the beef in 2 batches and cook until it's well browned on all sides, stirring often. Remove the beef with a slotted spoon and set it aside.

2. Reduce the heat to medium and add the remaining oil. Add the onion. Cook and stir until the onion is tender. Add garlic and cook for 30 seconds.

3. Add the salsa, water, chili powder, cumin and beans. Heat to a boil. Return the beef to the saucepot. Reduce the heat to low. Cover and cook for 1 hour. Uncover and cook for 30 minutes more or until beef is fork-tender. Sprinkle with cilantro and serve with *Chili Toppings*, if desired.

Makes: 6 servings

Moroccan Lamb Stew

START TO FINISH: 1 hour 50 minutes

Prepping: 15 minutes
Cooking: 1 hour 35 minutes

1. Heat the oil in a 4-quart saucepot over medium-high heat. Add the lamb in 2 batches and cook until it's well browned on all sides, stirring often. Remove lamb with a slotted spoon and put it in a medium bowl. Sprinkle the cinnamon and cloves over the lamb and stir until lightly coated.

2. Reduce the heat to medium. Add the onion. Cook and stir until the onion is tender-crisp. Add the broth. Heat to a boil. Return the lamb to the saucepot. Reduce the heat to low. Cover and cook for 1 hour.

3. Add the lentils and potatoes. Cook for 20 minutes more or until the lentils and potatoes are tender. Serve with couscous topped with tomatoes and cilantro, if desired.

Makes: 8 servings

1 tablespoon olive oil
2 pounds lamb for stew,
   cut into 1-inch pieces
½ teaspoon ground
   cinnamon
¼ teaspoon ground cloves
1 medium onion, chopped
   (about ½ cup)
4 cups Swanson® Chicken
   Broth (Regular,
   Natural Goodness™ or
   Certified Organic)
1 cup dried lentils
2 medium potatoes, cut
   into cubes (about
   2 cups)
Hot cooked couscous
   (optional)
Chopped tomatoes
   (optional)
Chopped fresh cilantro
   leaves (optional)

Broccoli and Pasta Bianco

START TO FINISH: 45 minutes

Prepping: 20 minutes
Baking: 25 minutes

1. Prepare the pasta according to the package directions. Add the broccoli during the last 4 minutes of the cooking time. Drain the pasta and broccoli well in a colander.

2. Stir the soup, milk and black pepper in a 12×8×2-inch shallow baking dish. Stir in the pasta mixture, ¾ **cup** of the mozzarella cheese and **2 tablespoons** of the Parmesan cheese. Top with the remaining mozzarella and Parmesan cheeses.

3. Bake at 350°F. for 25 minutes or until hot and the cheese melts.

Makes: 8 servings

1 package (16 ounces) medium tube-shaped pasta (penne)
4 cups fresh **or** frozen broccoli flowerets
1 can (10¾ ounces) Campbell's® Condensed Cream of Mushroom Soup (Regular **or** 98% Fat Free)
1½ cups milk
½ teaspoon ground black pepper
1½ cups shredded mozzarella cheese (6 ounces)
¼ cup shredded Parmesan cheese

Family Favorites

Margarita Shrimp Salad

START TO FINISH: 55 minutes

Marinating: 30 minutes
Prepping: 15 minutes
Cooking: 10 minutes

1. Mix the lime juice, lime peel and garlic in a 12×8×2-inch nonmetallic shallow baking dish or gallon size resealable plastic bag. Add the shrimp and toss to coat with the marinade. Cover the dish or seal the plastic bag and refrigerate it for 30 minutes, turning the shrimp over a few times while it's marinating.

2. Heat the broth in a 2-quart saucepan over high heat to a boil. Add the pepper and onion and cook until the vegetables are tender-crisp.

3. Reduce the heat to medium. Add the shrimp and marinade. Cook until the shrimp turn pink. Stir in the cilantro. Divide the lettuce, tomatoes and shrimp mixture among 4 serving plates.

Makes: 4 servings

1 tablespoon lime juice
2 teaspoons grated lime peel
3 cloves garlic, minced
1 pound fresh large shrimp, shelled and deveined
¾ cup Swanson® Chicken Broth (Regular, Natural Goodness™ **or** Certified Organic)
1 medium orange **or** red pepper, cut into 2-inch-long strips (about 1½ cups)
1 small onion, sliced (about ¼ cup)
¼ cup chopped fresh cilantro leaves
4 cups torn romaine **or** iceberg lettuce
2 large tomatoes, thickly sliced

Family Favorites

1 can (10¾ ounces) Campbell's™ Condensed Cream of Mushroom Soup (Regular or 98% Fat Free)
1¼ cups water
½ cup milk
1½ cups frozen mixed vegetables
½ pound skinless, boneless chicken breasts, cut into cubes
¼ cup shredded part-skim mozzarella cheese
3 tablespoons grated Parmesan cheese
¾ cup uncooked Arborio or regular long-grain white rice

Baked Chicken & Cheese Risotto

START TO FINISH: 1 hour

Prepping: 10 minutes
Baking: 45 minutes
Standing: 5 minutes

1. Stir the soup, water, milk, vegetables, chicken, mozzarella cheese, Parmesan cheese and rice in a 13×9×2-inch shallow baking dish. Cover the dish with foil.

2. Bake at 400°F. for 35 minutes. Uncover the dish and stir.

3. Bake for 10 minutes more or until hot and the rice is tender. Let stand for 5 minutes.

Makes: 4 servings

Spiral Ham with Mango Salsa

START TO FINISH: 2 hours 15 minutes

Prepping: 15 minutes
Baking: 2 hours

1. Heat the butter in a 2-quart saucepan over medium-high heat. Add the onion and cook until it's tender. Stir in the broth, mango juice, dried mango and brown sugar. Heat to a boil. Reduce the heat to low. Cook for 10 minutes or until the mixture thickens. Let cool slightly.

2. Place a strainer over a medium bowl. Pour the broth mixture through the strainer. Reserve the broth mixture to glaze the ham. Put the strained mango mixture in a small bowl. Stir in the green onions. Cover and refrigerate until serving time.

3. Place the ham in a 17×11-inch roasting pan and cover loosely with foil. Bake at 325°F. for 1½ hours. Remove the foil. Spoon the broth mixture over the ham. Bake for 30 minutes more or until internal temperature of the ham reaches 140°F., basting the ham frequently with the pan drippings. Serve the ham with the mango salsa.

Makes: 24 servings

Easy Substitution Tip: Substitute chopped fresh cilantro leaves for the green onions.

1 tablespoon butter
1 medium onion, chopped (about ½ cup)
1½ cups Swanson® Chicken Broth (Regular, Natural Goodness™ **or** Certified Organic)
½ cup mango juice **or** nectar
1 package (6 ounces) dried mango, coarsely chopped
⅓ cup packed brown sugar
2 medium green onions, chopped (about ¼ cup)
9 pound fully cooked bone-in **or** 6 pound fully cooked boneless spiral cut ham

Barbecued Pork Spareribs

START TO FINISH: 55 minutes

Prepping: 15 minutes
Cooking/Grilling: 40 minutes

4 pounds pork spareribs
1 can (10¼ ounces)
    Campbell's™ Beef
    Gravy
¾ cup barbecue sauce
2 tablespoons packed
    brown sugar

1. Cut the ribs into serving pieces. Heat the ribs in a 4-quart saucepot over high heat in water to cover until the water boils. Reduce the heat to low. Cover and cook for 30 minutes until the meat is almost tender. Remove the ribs to paper towels to drain.

2. Mix the gravy, barbecue sauce and brown sugar in a large bowl. Add the ribs and toss gently to coat.

3. Lightly oil the grill rack. Preheat the grill. Grill the ribs over medium-hot coals for 10 minutes or until the meat is cooked through* and the ribs are glazed, turning the ribs over frequently during cooking and brushing with the gravy mixture occasionally.

Makes: 4 servings

The internal temperature of the pork should reach 160°F.

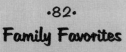

Fish & Vegetable Skillet

START TO FINISH: 25 minutes

Prepping: 5 minutes
Cooking: 20 minutes

1. Heat the water, wine, thyme, black pepper, celery and carrot in a 10-inch skillet over high heat to a boil. Reduce the heat to low. Cover and cook for 5 minutes or until the vegetables are tender-crisp.

2. Stir in the soup. Heat to a boil.

3. Place the fish in the soup mixture. Cover and cook for 5 minutes more or until the fish flakes easily when tested with a fork.

Makes: 4 servings

¼ cup water
2 tablespoons dry white wine
½ teaspoon dried thyme leaves, crushed
  Generous dash ground black pepper
2 stalks celery, cut into 2-inch-long sticks (about 1⅓ cups)
1 large carrot, cut into 2-inch-long sticks (about 1 cup)
1 small onion, chopped (about ¼ cup)
1 can (10¾ ounces) Campbell's® Condensed Cream of Mushroom Soup (Regular **or** 98% Fat Free)
1 pound fresh white fish fillets (cod, haddock **or** halibut)

**1½ pounds boneless beef sirloin or top round steak, 1½-inches thick
1 jar (16 ounces) Pace® Picante Sauce or Chunky Salsa**

Sirloin Steak Picante

START TO FINISH: 37 minutes

Prepping: 5 minutes
Grilling: 22 minutes
Standing: 10 minutes

1. Lightly oil the grill rack and heat the grill to medium. Grill the steak for 22 minutes for medium-rare* or to desired doneness, turning the steak over halfway through cooking and brushing often with **1 cup** of the picante sauce.

2. Let stand for 10 minutes before slicing.

3. Serve additional picante sauce with the steak.

Makes: 6 servings

The internal temperature of the steak should reach 145°F.

Family Favorites

Sausage Stuffed Green Peppers

START TO FINISH: 1 hour

Prepping: 20 minutes
Baking: 40 minutes

1. Cut a thin slice from the top of each pepper, cut in half lengthwise and discard the seeds and white membranes. Place the pepper shells in a 13×9×2-inch shallow baking dish or roasting pan and set them aside.

2. Heat the oil in a 10-inch skillet over medium-high heat. Add the sausage and cook until it's well browned, stirring to break up the meat. Add the oregano and onion and cook until the onion is tender. Pour off any fat. Stir in the cheese.

3. Spoon the sausage mixture into the pepper shells. Pour the pasta sauce over the peppers. Cover. Bake at 400°F. for 40 minutes or until sausage reaches an internal temperature of 160°F. and the peppers are tender.

Makes: 8 servings

- 4 medium green peppers
- 1 tablespoon vegetable oil
- 1 pound sweet Italian pork sausage, casing removed
- 1 teaspoon dried oregano leaves, crushed
- 1 medium onion, chopped (about ½ cup)
- 1 cup shredded part-skim mozzarella cheese (4 ounces)
- 2 cups Prego® Traditional Pasta Sauce

Family Favorites

Chicken Broccoli Divan

START TO FINISH: 40 minutes

Prepping: 15 minutes
Baking: 25 minutes

1. Arrange the broccoli and chicken in a 9-inch pie plate or 2-quart shallow baking dish.

2. Mix the soup and milk in a small bowl and pour over the broccoli and chicken mixture. Sprinkle the cheese over the soup mixture. Mix bread crumbs with the butter and sprinkle over the cheese.

3. Bake at 400°F. for 25 minutes or until hot and bubbly and bread crumbs are browned.

Makes: 4 servings

Easy Substitution Tip: Substitute 1 can (10¾ ounces) Campbell's® Condensed Cream of Chicken Soup (Regular **or** 98% Fat Free) for the Broccoli Cheese Soup.

1 pound fresh broccoli, cut into spears **or** 1 package (about 10 ounces) frozen broccoli spears, cooked and drained
1½ cups cubed cooked chicken **or** turkey
1 can (10¾ ounces) Campbell's® Condensed Broccoli Cheese Soup (Regular **or** 98% Fat Free)
⅓ cup milk
½ cup shredded Cheddar cheese (optional)
2 tablespoons dry bread crumbs
1 tablespoon butter, melted

Family Favorites

Creamy 3-Cheese Pasta

START TO FINISH: 40 minutes

Prepping: 20 minutes
Baking: 20 minutes

1. Stir the soup, milk, black pepper and cheeses in a 1½-quart casserole dish. Stir in the pasta.

2. Bake at 400°F. for 20 minutes or until hot.

3. Stir before serving.

Makes: 4 servings

1 can (10¾ ounces) Campbell's® Condensed Cream of Mushroom Soup (Regular or 98% Fat Free)
1 cup milk
¼ teaspoon ground black pepper
1 package (8 ounces) shredded two-cheese blend
⅓ cup grated Parmesan cheese
3 cups corkscrew-shaped pasta (rotelle), cooked and drained

3 teaspoons butter
8 filet mignons (tenderloin steaks), ¾-inch thick (about 5 ounces **each**)
½ cup chopped shallots **or** onion
1 clove garlic, minced
1 can (10¼ ounces) Campbell's™ Beef Gravy
½ cup dry red wine

Pan-Seared Beef Steaks with Garlic Red Wine Gravy

START TO FINISH: 25 minutes

Prepping: 10 minutes
Cooking: 15 minutes

1. Heat **1 teaspoon** butter in a 12-inch skillet over high heat. Add **4** steaks and cook for 2 minutes on each side for medium-rare* or to desired doneness. Remove the steaks. Cover and keep warm. Repeat with **1 teaspoon** butter and the remaining steaks.

2. Reduce the heat to medium, add the remaining butter. Add the shallots and cook for 1 minute. Add the garlic and cook for 30 seconds.

3. Stir in the gravy and wine. Heat to a boil. Return the steaks to the skillet and heat through.

Makes: 8 servings

The internal temperature of the steaks should reach 145°F.

Cheesy Chicken and Rice Bake

START TO FINISH: 50 minutes

Prepping: 5 minutes
Baking: 45 minutes

1. Mix the soup, water, rice, onion powder and black pepper in a 2-quart shallow baking dish. Top with chicken and sprinkle chicken with additional black pepper.

2. Cover and bake at 375°F. for 45 minutes or until chicken is cooked through* and rice is done.

3. Uncover and sprinkle cheese over the chicken.

Makes: 4 to 6 servings

*The internal temperature of the chicken should reach 160°F.

1 can (10¾ ounces)
  Campbell's® Cream of
  Chicken Soup (Regular
  or 98% Fat Free)
1⅓ cups water
¾ cup **uncooked** regular
  long-grain white rice
½ teaspoon onion powder
¼ teaspoon ground black
  pepper
1½ pounds skinless,
  boneless chicken
  breast halves
  (about 4-6)
1 cup shredded Cheddar
  cheese (4 ounces)

Ranchero Beef Taco Bake

START TO FINISH: 40 minutes

Prepping: 10 minutes
Baking: 30 minutes

1. Cook the beef in a 10-inch skillet over medium-high heat until the beef is well browned, stirring frequently to break up meat. Pour off any fat.

2. Add the soup, salsa, water, tortillas and ⅓ **cup** of the cheese. Spoon into a 12×8×2-inch shallow baking dish. Cover the dish with foil.

3. Bake at 400°F. for 30 minutes or until hot. Sprinkle with the remaining cheese.

Makes: 5 servings

Easy Substitution Tip: Substitute ground turkey for the ground beef.

1 pound ground beef
1 can (10¾ ounces) Campbell's® Condensed Creamy Ranchero Tomato Soup
¾ cup Pace® Chunky Salsa
¾ cup water
8 corn tortillas **or** 6 flour tortillas (6-to 8-inch), cut into 1-inch pieces
⅔ cup shredded Cheddar cheese

Chicken Nacho Tacos

START TO FINISH: 25 minutes

Prepping: 10 minutes
Cooking: 15 minutes

1. Heat the oil in a 10-inch skillet over medium heat. Add the onion and chili powder and cook until the onion is tender.

2. Stir in the soup and chicken. Cook and stir until it's hot.

3. Divide the chicken mixture among the taco shells. Top with the lettuce and tomato.

Makes: 8 tacos

1 tablespoon vegetable oil
1 medium onion, chopped (about ½ cup)
½ teaspoon chili powder
1 can (11 ounces) Campbell's® Condensed Fiesta Nacho Cheese Soup
2 cans (4.5 ounces **each**) Swanson® Premium Chunk Chicken Breast, drained
8 taco shells **or** flour tortillas (6 inch), warmed
Shredded lettuce **and** chopped tomato

Holiday Fun

German Potato Salad

START TO FINISH: 1 hour 5 minutes

Prepping: 20 minutes
Cooking: 30 minutes
Cooling: 15 minutes

10 medium potatoes (about 3 pounds)
3 tablespoons chopped fresh parsley
¼ cup all-purpose flour
1¾ cups Swanson® Beef Broth (Regular, Lower Sodium **or** Certified Organic)
¼ cup cider vinegar
3 tablespoons sugar
½ teaspoon celery seed
⅛ teaspoon ground black pepper
1 medium onion, chopped (about ½ cup)

1. Put the potatoes in a 3-quart saucepan with enough water to cover them. Heat the potatoes over medium-high heat to a boil. Reduce the heat to low. Cover and cook the potatoes for 20 minutes or until they're fork-tender. Drain the potatoes well in a colander. Let cool for 15 minutes or until potatoes are cool enough to handle and cut them into cubes.

2. Mix the potatoes and parsley in a 3-quart bowl.

3. Stir the flour with the broth, vinegar, sugar, celery seed and black pepper in a 2-quart saucepan. Stir in the onion. Heat the mixture to a boil over medium-high heat. Reduce the heat to low. Cook and stir for 5 minutes or until the onion is tender and the mixture boils and thickens. Pour over the potato mixture, tossing until well coated. Serve the salad warm.

Makes: 12 servings

1 can (10¾ ounces)
Campbell's®
Condensed Cream of
Mushroom Soup
(Regular **or** 98% Fat
Free)
½ cup milk
1 teaspoon soy sauce
Dash ground black
pepper
2 packages (10 ounces
each) frozen cut
green beans, cooked
and drained
1 can (2.8 ounces) french
fried onions (1⅓ cups)

Green Bean Casserole

START TO FINISH: 40 minutes

Prepping: 10 minutes
Baking: 30 minutes

1. Stir the soup, milk, soy, black pepper, green beans and ⅔ **cup** onions in a 1½-quart casserole.

2. Bake at 350°F. for 25 minutes or until hot. Stir the green bean mixture.

3. Sprinkle the remaining onions over the green bean mixture. Bake for 5 minutes more or until onions are golden brown.

Makes: 5 servings

Roasted Asparagus with Lemon & Goat Cheese

START TO FINISH: 30 minutes

Prepping: 10 minutes
Roasting: 20 minutes

1. Heat the oven to 425°F. Spray a 17×11-inch roasting pan or shallow baking sheet with cooking spray.

2. Stir the asparagus and oil in the prepared pan. Season with the black pepper. Pour in the broth.

3. Roast the asparagus for 20 minutes or until the asparagus is fork-tender, stirring once. Top with the cheese, lemon juice and lemon peel.

Makes: 6 servings

Vegetable cooking spray
2 pounds asparagus, trimmed
1 tablespoon olive oil
Freshly ground black pepper
½ cup Swanson® Vegetable Broth (Regular or Certified Organic)
3 ounces soft goat cheese, crumbled
1 tablespoon lemon juice
1 teaspoon grated lemon peel

4 teaspoons cornstarch
2 tablespoons water
1 tablespoon sesame oil
8 cups Swanson® Chicken Broth (Regular, Natural Goodness™ or Certified Organic)
3 tablespoons soy sauce
2 eggs, beaten
1 package (16 ounces) thin spaghetti, cooked and drained
¼ pound sliced cooked ham, cut into 2-inch-long strips (about 1 cup)
4 medium green onions, chopped (about ½ cup)

Longevity Noodles

START TO FINISH: 25 minutes

Prepping: 10 minutes
Cooking: 15 minutes

1. Stir the cornstarch, water and sesame oil in a small cup. Set the mixture aside.

2. Heat the broth and soy in a 3-quart saucepan over medium-high heat to a boil. Stir the cornstarch mixture and stir it into the saucepan. Cook and stir until mixture is slightly thickened.

3. Reduce the heat to low. Add the eggs, in a slow steady stream, stirring while adding. Remove the saucepan from the heat. Divide the pasta, ham and green onions among 8 serving bowls. Ladle **about 1 cup** broth mixture into each bowl. Serve immediately.

Makes: 8 servings

Holiday Fun

Cheesy Mexican Cornbread

START TO FINISH: 50 minutes

Prepping: 15 minutes
Baking: 20 minutes
Cooling: 15 minutes

1. Heat the oven to 450°F. Pour **1 tablespoon** melted butter into a 9-inch round cake pan. Set the pan aside.

2. Mix the cornmeal, flour, sugar and baking powder in 2-quart bowl. Beat the soup, milk, egg and remaining melted butter in a 1-quart bowl with fork or whisk until the ingredients are mixed. Stir the soup mixture into the cornmeal mixture with a fork just until the dry ingredients are moistened. Stir in the corn. Pour the batter into the prepared pan.

3. Bake for 20 minutes or until a toothpick inserted in the center of the bread comes out clean. Remove the pan from the oven and place on wire rack. Sprinkle with the cheese. Let cool for 15 minutes. Cut into 8 wedges. Serve warm.

Makes: 8 servings

Easy Substitution Tip: Substitute 1 cup frozen whole kernel corn, thawed, for the canned corn.

3 tablespoons butter, melted
1 cup yellow cornmeal
¾ cup all-purpose flour
⅓ cup sugar
1 tablespoon baking powder
1 can (10¾ ounces) Campbell's® Condensed Cheddar Cheese Soup
½ cup milk
1 egg, beaten
1 can (about 8 ounces) whole kernel corn, drained
½ cup shredded Cheddar cheese

8 medium potatoes,
    (about 3 pounds),
    peeled and grated
    (about 7 cups)
2 cans (10¾ ounces **each**)
    Campbell's®
    **Condensed Broccoli
    Cheese Soup (Regular
    or 98% Fat Free)**
3 eggs, beaten
2 tablespoons all-purpose
    flour
¼ teaspoon freshly ground
    black pepper
½ cup vegetable oil
    Sour cream
    Chopped chives

Holiday Potato Pancakes

START TO FINISH: 55 minutes

Prepping: 25 minutes
Cooking: 30 minutes

1. Wrap the grated potatoes in a clean dish or paper towel. Twist the towel and squeeze to wring out as much of the liquid as possible.

2. Mix the soup, eggs, flour, black pepper and potatoes in a 3-quart bowl.

3. Heat ¼ **cup** oil in a deep nonstick 12-inch skillet over medium-high heat. Drop a scant ¼ **cup** potato mixture into the pan, making **4** pancakes at a time. Press on each pancake to flatten to 3 or 4 inches. Cook for 4 minutes, turning once or until the pancakes are dark golden brown. Remove the pancakes and keep warm. Repeat with the remaining potato mixture, adding more of the remaining oil as needed. Serve with the sour cream and chives.

Makes: 36 pancakes

Eggplant Tomato Gratin

START TO FINISH: 55 minutes

Prepping: 20 minutes
Baking: 25 minutes
Standing: 10 minutes

1. Heat the oven to 425°F. Spray a baking sheet with cooking spray. Arrange the eggplant on the sheet in a single layer. Bake for 20 minutes or until the eggplant is tender, turning halfway through baking. Spray a 13×9×2-inch shallow baking dish with cooking spray.

2. Stir the soup, milk and cheese in a 1-quart bowl. Put **half** the eggplant, tomatoes, onion, basil and soup mixture in the prepared dish. Repeat the layers. Mix the bread crumbs and parsley with the oil in a small bowl. Sprinkle the bread crumb mixture over the soup mixture.

3. Reduce the oven temperature to 400°F. Bake for 25 minutes or until hot and topping is golden brown. Let stand for 10 minutes before serving.

Makes: 8 servings

Make Ahead Tip: Can be prepared ahead up to topping with bread crumb mixture. Cover and refrigerate overnight. Uncover and sprinkle with the bread crumb mixture. Bake at 400°F. for 30 minutes or until hot and golden brown.

Vegetable cooking spray
1 large eggplant (about 1¼ pounds), cut into ½-inch-thick slices
1 can (10¾ ounces) Campbell's® Condensed Cream of Celery Soup (Regular **or** 98% Fat Free)
½ cup milk
¼ cup grated Parmesan cheese
2 large tomatoes, cut into ½-inch-thick slices (about 2 cups)
1 medium onion, thinly sliced (about ½ cup)
¼ cup chopped fresh basil leaves
¼ cup Italian-seasoned dry bread crumbs
1 tablespoon chopped fresh parsley (optional)
1 tablespoon olive oil

1¾ cups Swanson® Chicken
Broth (Regular,
Natural Goodness™ **or**
Certified Organic)
3 tablespoons lemon juice
1 teaspoon dried basil
leaves, crushed
1 teaspoon dried thyme
leaves, crushed
⅛ teaspoon ground black
pepper
12- to 14-pound turkey
2 cans (14½ ounces **each**)
Campbell's™ Turkey
Gravy

Holiday Fun

Herb Roasted Turkey

START TO FINISH: 4 to 4½ hours 55 minutes

Prepping: 15 minutes
Roasting: 4 to 4½ hours 30 minutes
Standing: 10 minutes

1. Mix the broth, lemon juice, basil, thyme and black pepper in a medium bowl.

2. Roast the turkey according to package directions*, basting occasionally with the broth mixture. Let the turkey stand for 10 minutes before slicing. Discard any remaining broth mixture.

3. Heat the gravy and serve with the turkey.

Makes: 12 to 14 servings

The internal temperature of the turkey should reach 180°F.

Heavenly Sweet Potatoes

START TO FINISH: 30 minutes

Prepping: 10 minutes
Baking: 20 minutes

1. Spray a 1½-quart casserole with cooking spray. Set the dish aside.

2. Place the potatoes, cinnamon and ginger in a 3-quart bowl. Beat with an electric mixer on medium speed until the potatoes are fluffy and almost smooth. Add the broth and beat until the ingredients are mixed. Spoon the potato mixture into the prepared dish. Top with the marshmallows.

3. Bake at 350°F. for 20 minutes or until hot and marshmallows are golden brown.

Makes: 8 servings

Vegetable cooking spray
1 can (40 ounces) cut
   sweet potatoes in
   heavy syrup, drained
¼ teaspoon ground
   cinnamon
⅛ teaspoon ground ginger
¾ cup Swanson® Chicken
   Broth (Regular,
   Natural Goodness™ **or**
   Certified Organic)
2 cups miniature
   marshmallows

Holiday Fun

2 tablespoons butter
1 small onion, chopped (about ¼ cup)
¾ cup Swanson® Chicken Broth (Regular, Natural Goodness™ or Certified Organic)
1 tablespoon packed brown sugar
¼ teaspoon dried thyme leaves, crushed
⅛ teaspoon ground black pepper
1 pumpkin **or** calabaza squash (about 2½ pounds), peeled, seeded and cut into 1-inch pieces (about 5 to 6 cups)
2 medium Macintosh apples, peeled, cored and cut into 1-inch pieces

Pumpkin Apple Mash

START TO FINISH: 30 minutes

Prepping: 5 minutes
Cooking: 25 minutes

1. Heat the butter in a 3-quart saucepan over medium heat. Add the onion and cook until the onion is tender.

2. Add the broth, brown sugar, thyme, black pepper and pumpkin to the saucepan. Heat to a boil. Reduce the heat to low. Cover and cook for 10 minutes or until the pumpkin is tender.

3. Add the apples. Cook for 5 minutes more or until the apples are tender. Mash lightly with a fork or potato masher. Serve immediately.

Makes: 4 servings

Layered Cranberry Walnut Stuffing

START TO FINISH: 35 minutes

Prepping: 10 minutes
Baking: 25 minutes

1. Prepare the stuffing using the broth and butter according to the package directions.

2. Spoon **half** of the stuffing into a 2-quart casserole. Spoon **half** of the cranberry sauce over the stuffing. Sprinkle with ¼ **cup** walnuts. Repeat the layers.

3. Bake at 350°F. for 25 minutes or until hot.

Makes: 6 servings

2 boxes (6 ounces **each**)
 Pepperidge Farm®
 Stuffing Mix
1½ cups Swanson® Chicken
 Broth (Regular,
 Natural Goodness™
 or Certified Organic)
2 tablespoons butter
1 can (16 ounces) whole
 cranberry sauce
½ cup walnuts, toasted
 and chopped

Lemon Herb Broccoli Casserole

1 can (10¾ ounces)
    Campbell's®
    Condensed Cream of
    Chicken with Herbs
    Soup
½ cup milk
1 tablespoon lemon juice
1 bag (16 ounces) frozen
    broccoli cuts, thawed
    (about 4 cups)
1 can (2.8 ounces) french
    fried onions (1⅓ cups)

START TO FINISH: 40 minutes

Prepping: 10 minutes
Baking: 30 minutes

1. Stir the soup, milk, lemon juice, broccoli and ⅔ **cup** onions in a 1½-quart casserole and cover.

2. Bake at 350°F. for 25 minutes or until the broccoli is tender. Stir the broccoli mixture.

3. Sprinkle the remaining onions over the broccoli mixture. Bake for 5 minutes more or until the onions are golden brown.

Makes: 6 servings

Time-Saving Tip: To thaw the broccoli, cut off 1 corner on bag, microwave on HIGH for 3 minutes.

Swiss Vegetable Bake

START TO FINISH: 50 minutes

Prepping: 5 minutes
Baking: 45 minutes

1. Stir the soup, sour cream, black pepper, vegetables, **1½ cups** cheese and **1⅓ cups** onions in a 13×9×2-inch shallow baking dish and cover.

2. Bake at 350°F. for 40 minutes or until the vegetables are tender. Stir the vegetable mixture.

3. Sprinkle the remaining cheese and onions over the vegetable mixture. Bake for 5 minutes more or until the onions are golden brown.

Makes: 8 servings

Time-Saving Tip: To thaw the vegetables, cut off 1 corner on bag, microwave on HIGH for 5 minutes.

1 can (26 ounces) Campbell's® Condensed Cream of Chicken Soup
⅔ cup sour cream
½ teaspoon ground black pepper
2 bags (16 ounces **each**) frozen vegetable combination (broccoli, cauliflower, carrots), thawed
2 cups shredded Swiss cheese (8 ounces)
1 can (6 ounces) french fried onions (2⅔ cups)

1 can (10¾ ounces)
  Campbell's®
  Condensed Cheddar
  Cheese Soup
¼ cup milk
1 tablespoon butter,
  melted
  Dash ground red pepper
1 bag (16 ounces) frozen
  whole kernel corn,
  thawed (about 3 cups)
1 can (4 ounces) Pace®
  Diced Green Chilies
1 can (2.8 ounces) french
  fried onions (1⅓ cups)

Cheesy Chile Corn Casserole

START TO FINISH: 40 minutes

Prepping: 10 minutes
Baking: 30 minutes

1. Stir the soup, milk, butter, pepper, corn, chilies and ⅔ **cup** onions in a 1½-quart casserole.

2. Bake at 350°F. for 25 minutes. Stir the vegetable mixture.

3. Sprinkle the remaining onions over the vegetable mixture. Bake for 5 minutes more or until the onions are golden brown.

Makes: 6 servings

Holiday Fun

Loaded Baked Potato Casserole

START TO FINISH: 50 minutes

Prepping: 15 minutes
Baking: 35 minutes

1. Stir the potatoes, **1⅓ cups** onions, peas, cheese and bacon in a 13×9×2-inch shallow baking dish. Mix the soup and milk in a 1-quart bowl and pour over the potato mixture. Cover the dish.

2. Bake at 350°F. for 30 minutes or until hot. Uncover the dish and stir the potato mixture.

3. Sprinkle with the remaining onions. Bake for 5 minutes more or until onions are golden brown.

Makes: 8 servings

Time-Saving Tip: To thaw the hash browns, cut off 1 corner on bag, microwave on HIGH for 5 minutes.

1 bag (32 ounces) frozen Southern-style hash brown potatoes, thawed (about 7½ cups)
1 can (6 ounces) french fried onions (2⅔ cups)
1 cup frozen peas, thawed
1 cup shredded Cheddar cheese (4 ounces)
4 slices bacon, cooked and crumbled
2 cans (10¾ ounces **each**) Campbell's® Condensed Cream of Celery Soup (Regular or 98% Fat Free)
1 cup milk

Holiday Fun

4 tablespoons butter, melted
¼ cup sugar
2 teaspoons grated orange peel
1 teaspoon ground cinnamon
1½ cups Pepperidge Farm® Corn Bread Stuffing
½ cup pecan halves, coarsely chopped
1 can (16 ounces) whole berry cranberry sauce
⅓ cup orange juice **or** water
4 large cooking apples, cored and thinly sliced (about 6 cups)

Holiday Fun

Scalloped Apple Bake

START TO FINISH: 1 hour 5 minutes

Prepping: 25 minutes
Baking: 40 minutes

1. Mix the butter, sugar, orange peel, cinnamon, stuffing and pecans in a 1-quart bowl. Set the mixture aside.

2. Mix the cranberry sauce, juice and apples in a 3-quart bowl. Add ½ of the stuffing mixture and stir lightly to coat. Spoon into an 8-inch square baking dish. Sprinkle the remaining stuffing mixture over the apple mixture.

3. Bake at 375°F. for 40 minutes or until the apples are tender.

Makes: 6 servings

Baked Eyeballs Casserole

START TO FINISH: 50 minutes

Prepping: 15 minutes
Baking: 25 minutes
Standing: 10 minutes

1. Spray a 13×9×2-inch shallow baking dish with the cooking spray.

2. Mix **1½ cups** pasta sauce, ricotta cheese, **½ cup** Parmesan cheese and pasta in the prepared dish. Spread the remaining pasta sauce over the pasta mixture. Sprinkle with the remaining Parmesan cheese and cover with foil.

3. Bake at 400°F. for 25 minutes or until hot. Arrange the cheese balls randomly over the pasta mixture. Place a sliced olive on each cheese ball. Let stand for 10 minutes before serving.

Makes: 8 servings

Easy Substitution Tip: If fresh mozzarella balls are not available, substitute 1 package (8 ounces) fresh mozzarella. Cut crosswise into thirds. Cut each third in 6 wedges, for triangle-shaped eyes.

Vegetable cooking spray
1 jar (1 pound 11.5 ounces) Prego® Hearty Meat™ Italian Sausage Meat Sauce
1 container (15 ounces) part-skim ricotta cheese
¾ cup grated Parmesan cheese
7 cups bow tie-shaped pasta, cooked and drained
1 container (8 ounces) small fresh mozzarella balls (about 1-inch)
2 tablespoons sliced pitted ripe olives

24 sliced blanched almonds
   Red liquid **or** paste food
   coloring
2 packages (about 9
   ounces **each**)
   refrigerated fully
   cooked breaded
   chicken strips
   (about 24)
1 egg, slightly beaten
1 jar (1 pound 10 ounces)
   Prego® Traditional
   Pasta Sauce

Bloody Fingers

START TO FINISH: 20 minutes

Prepping: 15 minutes
Baking: 5 minutes

1. Heat the oven to 400°F. Brush the almonds with the food coloring to coat. Set them aside to dry, about 10 minutes.

2. Place the chicken strips on a baking sheet. Brush the narrow end of the chicken strips with egg and press almonds on the egg wash to attach. Bake for 5 minutes or until hot.

3. Pour the pasta sauce in a 2-quart saucepan over medium heat. Cook until it's hot and bubbling, stirring occasionally. Arrange the chicken on a serving platter. Serve with the sauce for dipping.

Makes: 8 servings

Easy Substitution Tip: Substitute frozen fully cooked breaded chicken strips for the refrigerated chicken strips. Increase the bake time to 10 minutes.

Holiday Fun

Freaky Pizza Fondue

START TO FINISH: 23 minutes

Prepping: 15 minutes
Cooking: 8 minutes

1. Place the pepper and pepperoni in a 1-quart microwavable dish. Cover and microwave on HIGH for 3 minutes or until the pepper is tender, stirring halfway through cooking.

2. Add the cream cheese and the Parmesan cheese and stir until it's smooth and well blended. Stir in the pasta sauce. Cover and microwave on HIGH for 5 minutes or until hot, stirring halfway through cooking.

3. Serve warm with the bread cubes for dipping.

Makes: About 3 cups

1 medium red **or** green pepper, chopped (about ¾ cup)
½ cup finely chopped pepperoni
½ of an 8 ounce package cream cheese, cut into cubes (about 1 cup)
⅓ cup grated Parmesan cheese
1¾ cups Prego® Traditional Pasta Sauce
1 loaf Italian bread (about 1 pound), cut into cubes

½ of a 17.3 ounce package
  Pepperidge Farm®
  Frozen Puff Pastry
  Sheets (1 sheet)
1 package (14 ounces)
  cocktail franks
  (about 30)
¼ cup prepared mustard
¼ cup ketchup

Goblin's Toes

START TO FINISH: 1 hour 10 minutes

Thawing: 40 minutes
Prepping: 10 minutes
Baking: 20 minutes

1. Thaw the pastry sheet at room temperature for 40 minutes or until it's easy to handle. Heat the oven 375°F. Lightly grease a baking sheet.

2. Unfold the pastry sheet on a lightly floured surface. Cut it in half lengthwise. Cut each half crosswise into 15 (½-inch-wide) strips. Wrap one end of each cocktail frank with one pastry strip, overlapping slightly to resemble a "bandage." Put them on a baking sheet about 1 inch apart.

3. Bake for 20 minutes or until the pastry is golden. Remove the cocktail franks from the baking sheet and cool them slightly on a wire rack. Dollop some mustard on toes. Serve with remaining mustard and ketchup for dipping.

Makes: 30 appetizers

Holiday Fun

October Dinner Fondue

START TO FINISH: 15 minutes

Prepping: 5 minutes
Cooking: 10 minutes

1. Stir the soup and milk in a 2-quart saucepan. Heat over medium heat until hot, stirring occasionally. Add the cheese. Cook and stir until the cheese melts. Stir in the cilantro.

2. Pour the soup mixture into a fondue pot.

3. Serve warm with the *Suggested Dippers*.

Makes: 2 cups

1 can (10¾ ounces) Campbell's® Condensed Southwest Pepper Jack Soup
¾ cup milk
1 cup shredded Cheddar cheese (4 ounces)
2 tablespoons chopped fresh cilantro leaves

Suggested Dippers: Cooked breaded chicken nuggets, cooked shrimp, tortellini, mini ravioli, French fries, steamed fresh vegetables (cauliflower, broccoli, green beans **or** zucchini)

Holiday Fun

Vegetables and Sides

Crab and Asparagus Risotto

2 tablespoons olive oil

1 medium orange pepper, diced (about 1 cup)

½ cup chopped onion **or** shallots

2 cups **uncooked** Arborio rice (short-grain)

½ cup dry white wine

6 cups Swanson® Chicken Broth (Regular, Natural Goodness™ **or** Certified Organic), heated

½ pound asparagus **or** green beans, trimmed, cut into 1-inch pieces (about 1½ cups)

½ pound refrigerated pasteurized crabmeat (about 1½ cups)

¼ cup grated Parmesan cheese

START TO FINISH: 35 minutes

Prepping/Cooking: 30 minutes
Standing: 5 minutes

1. Heat the oil in a 4-quart saucepan over medium heat. Add the pepper and onion and cook for 3 minutes or until the vegetables are tender. Add the rice and cook and stir for 2 minutes or until the rice is opaque.

2. Add the wine and cook and stir until it's absorbed. Stir **2 cups** of the hot broth into the rice mixture. Cook and stir until the broth is absorbed, maintaining the rice at a gentle simmer. Continue cooking and adding broth, ½ cup at a time, stirring until it's absorbed after each addition before adding more. Add the asparagus and crabmeat with the last broth addition.

3. Stir the cheese into the risotto. Remove the saucepan from the heat. Cover and let it stand for 5 minutes. Serve the risotto with additional cheese.

Makes: 8 servings

4 teaspoons cornstarch
1¾ cups Swanson®
Vegetable Broth
(Regular or Certified
Organic)
4 medium carrots, sliced
(about 2 cups)
1 medium onion, chopped
(about ½ cup)
¾ pound snow peas
1 teaspoon lemon juice

Glazed Snow Peas and Carrots

START TO FINISH: 25 minutes

Prepping: 10 minutes
Cooking: 15 minutes

1. Stir the cornstarch and **1 cup** broth in a small cup. Set the mixture aside.

2. Heat the remaining broth in a 10-inch skillet over medium-high heat to a boil. Add the carrots and onion and reduce the heat to low. Cover and cook for 5 minutes or until the carrots are tender-crisp. Add the snow peas and cook for 2 minutes.

3. Stir the cornstarch mixture and stir it into the skillet. Cook and stir until the mixture boils and thickens. Stir in the lemon juice.

Makes: 8 servings

Vegetables and Sides

Mediterranean Chop Salad

START TO FINISH: 25 minutes

Prepping: 25 minutes

1. Mix the lettuce, cucumber, celery, red pepper, olives and croutons in a 4-quart serving bowl.
2. Pour the dressing over the vegetables, tossing until well coated.
3. Serve immediately with the black pepper and cheese.

Makes: 8 to 10 servings

1 package (12 ounces) romaine lettuce hearts, chopped
1 large seedless cucumber, peeled and chopped (about 1⅔ cups)
3 stalks celery, sliced **or** 1 cup sliced fennel (about 1½ cups)
1 cup chopped roasted red **or** yellow sweet peppers
½ cup chopped pitted ripe olives
1 box (6 ounces) Pepperidge Farm® Croutons, any variety
½ cup prepared balsamic vinaigrette dressing
Freshly ground black pepper
Parmesan cheese shavings

Vegetables and Sides

1 tablespoon olive oil
1 cup fresh **or** drained, canned whole kernel corn
1 large orange **or** red pepper, chopped (about 1 cup)
1 medium onion, chopped (about ½ cup)
1¾ cups **uncooked** regular long-grain white rice
4 cups Swanson® Chicken, Natural Goodness™ Chicken **or** Vegetable Broth
1 teaspoon ground sage
1 can (10¾ ounces) Campbell's® Condensed Cream of Celery Soup (Regular **or** 98% Fat Free)
¼ cup grated Parmesan cheese

Toasted Corn & Sage Harvest Risotto

START TO FINISH: 50 minutes

Prepping: 15 minutes
Cooking: 35 minutes

1. Heat the oil in a 4-quart saucepan over medium heat. Add the corn, pepper and onion and cook for 6 minutes or until the vegetables start to brown.

2. Add the rice and cook for 30 seconds, stirring constantly. Stir in the broth and sage and heat to a boil. Reduce the heat to low. Cover the saucepan and cook for 20 minutes or until the rice is done and most of the liquid is absorbed.

3. Stir in the soup. Cook for 2 minutes more, stirring occasionally until heated through. Sprinkle with cheese.

Makes: 16 servings

Vegetables and Sides

Harvest Salad

START TO FINISH: 10 minutes

Prepping: 10 minutes

1. Mix the salad greens and vegetables in a 3-quart bowl.

2. Beat the soup, oil, vinegar, honey and salad dressing mix with a whisk or fork in a 1-quart bowl. Pour ¾ **cup** of the soup mixture over the salad mixture, tossing until lightly coated.

3. Arrange the dressed salad mixture on a serving platter. Top with the croutons and seeds. Serve immediately with the remaining soup mixture.

Makes: 8 servings

2 packages (about 7 ounces **each**) mixed salad greens (8 cups)

2 cups cut-up fresh vegetables (red onion, cucumber and carrot)

1 can (10¾ ounces) Campbell's® Condensed Tomato Soup

¼ cup vegetable oil

¼ cup red wine vinegar

1 tablespoon honey **or** sugar

1 package (0.7 ounces) Italian salad dressing mix

1 box (5.5 ounces) Pepperidge Farm® Generous Cut Croutons, any variety

¼ cup shelled pumpkin **or** sunflower seeds

Vegetables and Sides

Mixed Greens and Fruit Salad with Warm Onion Vinaigrette

3 tablespoons olive oil

¼ cup finely chopped shallots **or** sweet onion

1 cup Swanson® Chicken Broth (Regular, Natural Goodness™ **or** Certified Organic)

2 tablespoons balsamic vinegar

¼ cup packed brown sugar

1 tablespoon coarse-grain Dijon-style mustard

2 bags (5 to 8 ounces **each**) mixed baby salad greens

2 ripe pears **or** crisp apples, cored and thinly sliced (about 2 cups)

½ cup dried cherries **or** cranberries

¼ cup pecans, toasted

Crumbled blue cheese (optional)

START TO FINISH: 20 minutes

Prepping: 20 minutes

1. Heat **1 tablespoon** of the oil in a 2-quart saucepan over medium heat. Add the shallots and cook for 3 minutes or until the shallots are tender.

2. Stir the broth, vinegar, brown sugar and mustard into the shallots. Heat the mixture to a boil. Cook for 5 minutes or until the mixture is slightly reduced. Remove the saucepan from the heat. Beat the remaining oil into the dressing mixture with a whisk. Let the dressing cool slightly.

3. Toss the salad greens with ½ **cup** of the dressing in a large bowl. Arrange the dressed greens on a serving platter. Top with the pears, cherries, pecans and blue cheese, if desired. Serve the salad with the remaining dressing.

Makes: 8 servings

Spaghetti Squash Alfredo

START TO FINISH: 1 hour 10 minutes

Prepping: 10 minutes
Baking/Cooking: 1 hour

1. Pierce squash with fork or skewer in several places. Bake at 350°F. for 50 minutes or until the squash is fork-tender. Cut in half, scoop out and discard seeds. Scrape the flesh with fork to separate the spaghetti-like strands.

2. Stir the soup, water and milk in a 2-quart saucepan. Heat over medium heat to a boil. Stir in the Swiss cheese.

3. Place the hot spaghetti squash in a 2-quart serving bowl. Pour the soup mixture over the squash. Toss to coat. Sprinkle with Parmesan cheese and parsley.

Makes: 5 servings

1 medium spaghetti squash (about 3 pounds)
1 can (10¾ ounces) Campbell's® Condensed Cream of Celery Soup (Regular or 98% Fat Free)
¾ cup water
¼ cup milk
1 cup shredded low fat Swiss cheese (4 ounces)
2 tablespoons grated Parmesan cheese
Chopped fresh parsley or chives

Vegetables and Sides

Broccoli & Noodles Supreme

3 cups **uncooked** medium egg noodles

2 cups broccoli flowerets

1 can (10¾ ounces) **Campbell's® Condensed Cream of Chicken Soup (Regular or 98% Fat Free)**

½ cup sour cream

⅓ cup grated Parmesan cheese

⅛ teaspoon ground black pepper

START TO FINISH: 30 minutes

Prepping: 10 minutes
Cooking: 20 minutes

1. Prepare the noodles according to the package directions in a 4-quart saucepot. Add the broccoli during the last 5 minutes of the cooking time. Drain the noodles and broccoli well in a colander and return them to the saucepot.

2. Stir the soup, sour cream, cheese and black pepper into the noodles and broccoli. Cook and stir over medium heat until hot.

3. Top with additional cheese before serving.

Makes: 5 servings

Vegetables and Sides

Mozzarella Zucchini Skillet

START TO FINISH: 25 minutes

Prepping: 10 minutes
Cooking: 15 minutes

1. Heat the oil in a 12-inch skillet over medium-high heat. Add the zucchini, onion and garlic powder and cook until the vegetables are tender-crisp.

2. Stir in the pasta sauce and heat through.

3. Sprinkle with the cheese. Cover and cook until the cheese melts.

Makes: 7 servings

2 tablespoons vegetable oil
5 medium zucchini, sliced (about 7½ cups)
1 medium onion, chopped (about ½ cup)
¼ teaspoon garlic powder **or 2 cloves garlic, minced**
1½ cups Prego® Traditional Pasta Sauce
½ cup shredded mozzarella **or Cheddar cheese**

Vegetables and Sides

Corn and Black-Eyed Pea Salad

START TO FINISH: 4 hours 15 minutes

Prepping: 15 minutes
Refrigerating: 4 hours

1. Mix the corn, peas, green pepper, red onion and cilantro in a 2-quart bowl. Stir the salsa into the corn mixture until well coated.

2. Cover and refrigerate the salad for 4 hours.

3. Stir the salad before serving.

Makes: 8 servings

Cooking for a Crowd: Recipe may be doubled.

Make Ahead Tip: Prepare the salad as directed. Cover and refrigerate the salad overnight. Stir the salad before serving.

1 bag (16 ounces) frozen whole kernel corn, thawed (about 3 cups)
1 can (16 ounces) black-eyed peas, rinsed and drained
1 large green pepper, chopped (about 1 cup)
½ cup chopped red onion
½ cup chopped fresh cilantro leaves
1 jar (16 ounces) Pace® Chunky Salsa

Vegetables and Sides

Oven-Roasted Root Vegetables

START TO FINISH: 1 hour 25 minutes

Prepping: 35 minutes
Roasting: 50 minutes

1. Heat the oven to 425°F. Spray a 17×11-inch roasting pan or shallow baking sheet with the cooking spray.

2. Stir the potatoes, carrots, celery root, rutabaga, onions, parsnips, garlic, rosemary and oil in the prepared pan. Roast the vegetables for 30 minutes. Pour the broth over the vegetables and stir.

3. Roast for 20 minutes more or until the vegetables are fork-tender.

Makes: 8 servings

Vegetable cooking spray
3 medium red potatoes (about 1 pound), cut into 1-inch pieces
2 cups fresh **or** frozen baby carrots
1 pound celery root, peeled and cut into 1-inch pieces (about 2 cups)
1 rutabaga (about 3 pounds), peeled and cut into 1-inch pieces (about 6 cups)
2 medium red onions, cut into 8 wedges **each**
2 medium parsnips, peeled and cut into 1-inch pieces (about 1½ cups)
5 cloves garlic, cut into thin slices
1 tablespoon chopped fresh rosemary **or** thyme **or** 1 teaspoon dried rosemary **or** thyme leaves, crushed
1 tablespoon olive oil
1 cup Swanson® Vegetable Broth (Regular **or** Certified Organic)

1 can (10¾ ounces)
    Campbell's®
    Condensed Cheddar
    Cheese Soup
½ cup milk
    Dash ground black
    pepper
4 cups cooked broccoli
    cuts
1 can (2.8 ounces) french
    fried onions (1⅓ cups)

Cheddar Broccoli Bake

START TO FINISH: 40 minutes

Prepping: 10 minutes
Baking: 30 minutes

1. Stir the soup, milk, black pepper, broccoli and ⅔ **cup** onions in a 1½-quart casserole and cover.

2. Bake at 350°F. for 25 minutes or until hot. Stir the broccoli mixture.

3. Sprinkle the remaining onions over the broccoli mixture. Bake for 5 minutes more or until the onions are golden.

Makes: 6 servings

Vegetables and Sides

Roasted Potatoes with Thyme

START TO FINISH: 45 minutes

Prepping: 10 minutes
Roasting: 35 minutes

1. Heat the oven to 400°F. Stir the potatoes, thyme, black pepper and oil in a 17×11-inch roasting pan or shallow baking sheet.

2. Roast the potatoes for 20 minutes. Turn the potatoes. Roast for 15 minutes more or until the potatoes are fork-tender and browned.

3. Heat the gravy and serve with the potatoes.

Makes: 4 servings

4 medium potatoes
   (about 1¼ pounds),
   sliced ¼-inch thick
1 teaspoon dried thyme
   leaves, crushed
¼ teaspoon ground black
   pepper
3 tablespoons vegetable
   oil
1 jar (12 ounces) Franco-
   American® Slow Roast
   Chicken Gravy

Vegetables and Sides

Sweet Treats

Apple Strudel

START TO FINISH: 2 hours 15 minutes

Thawing: 40 minutes
Prepping: 30 minutes
Baking: 35 minutes
Cooling: 30 minutes

½ of a 17.3 ounce package Pepperidge Farm® Frozen Puff Pastry Sheets (1 sheet)

1 egg

1 tablespoon water

2 tablespoons granulated sugar

1 tablespoon all-purpose flour

¼ teaspoon ground cinnamon

2 large Granny Smith apples, peeled, cored and thinly sliced

2 tablespoons raisins Confectioners' sugar (optional)

1. Thaw the pastry sheet at room temperature for 40 minutes or until it's easy to handle. Heat the oven to 375°F. Lightly grease a baking sheet. Stir the egg and water in a small bowl. Mix the sugar, flour and cinnamon in a medium bowl. Add the apples and raisins and toss to coat.

2. Unfold the pastry sheet on a lightly floured surface. Roll the sheet into a 16×12-inch rectangle. With the short side facing you, spoon the apple mixture on the bottom half of the pastry to within 1 inch of the edges. Starting at the short side closest to you, roll up like a jelly roll. Place seam-side down on the baking sheet. Tuck ends under to seal. Brush with the egg mixture. Cut several 2-inch-long slits 2 inches apart on the top.

3. Bake for 35 minutes or until golden. Cool on the baking sheet on a wire rack for 30 minutes. Slice and serve warm. Sprinkle with confectioners' sugar, if desired.

Makes: 6 servings

3 large sweet potatoes,
   peeled and cut into
   cubes (about 3 cups)
¼ cup heavy cream
1 can (10¾ ounces)
   Campbell's®
   Condensed Tomato
   Soup
1 cup packed brown sugar
3 eggs
1 teaspoon vanilla extract
½ teaspoon ground
   cinnamon
½ teaspoon ground
   nutmeg
1 (9-inch) unbaked pie
   crust

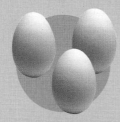

Sweet Potato Pie

START TO FINISH: 4 hours 45 minutes

Prepping: 15 minutes
Baking: 1 hour
Cooling: 3 hours 30 minutes

1. Heat the oven to 350°F. Put the potatoes in a 3-quart saucepan with enough water to cover them. Heat the potatoes over medium-high heat to a boil. Reduce the heat to low. Cover and cook the potatoes for 10 minutes or until they're fork-tender. Drain the potatoes well in a colander.

2. Place the potatoes in a 3-quart bowl. Add the cream. Beat the potatoes with an electric mixer at medium speed until the potatoes are fluffy and almost smooth. Add the soup, brown sugar, eggs, vanilla, cinnamon and nutmeg. Beat at low speed until the ingredients are mixed. Spoon the potato mixture into the prepared crust and place the pie plate on a baking sheet.

3. Bake for 1 hour or until the center is almost set. Cool the pie in the pan on a wire rack to room temperature.

Makes: 8 servings

Easy Substitution Tip: Substitute **1¾ cups** drained and mashed canned sweet potatoes for fresh mashed sweet potatoes. Beat with cream until fluffy and almost smooth.

Bread & Butter Pudding

START TO FINISH: 1 hour 5 minutes

Prepping: 20 minutes
Baking/Cooking: 40 minutes
Standing: 5 minutes

1. Heat the oven to 350°F. Grease a 13×9×2-inch shallow baking dish with some of the butter. Spread the remaining butter on the bread slices. Cut each bread slice in half diagonally. Layer ½ of the bread slices in the prepared dish. Sprinkle with ½ of the cinnamon and ½ of the currants. Repeat with the remaining bread slices, cinnamon and currants.

2. Beat the eggs, egg yolks and granulated sugar with a whisk or fork in a 3-quart bowl. Heat the cream and milk in a 2-quart saucepan over low heat until the mixture is warm. Stir in the vanilla. Stir some of the cream mixture into the egg mixture. Return the egg mixture to the saucepan. Pour over the bread. Let stand for 5 minutes. Sprinkle with the brown sugar.

3. Bake for 40 minutes or until the custard is set. Serve warm or at room temperature.

Makes: 8 servings

Time-Saving Tip: Substitute an 8 cup glass measuring cup for the saucepan. Pour the cream and milk in the cup. Microwave on MEDIUM (50% power) for about 7 minutes or until warm.

Make Ahead: Prepare the recipe through step 2 up to 1 day ahead but do not bake. Cover and refrigerate overnight. Bake at 350°F. for 40 minutes or until the custard is set.

1 stick butter (½ cup), softened
1 loaf (16 ounces) Pepperidge Farm® Toasting White Bread
2 teaspoons ground cinnamon
¼ cup currants
6 eggs
2 egg yolks
½ cup granulated sugar
4 cups heavy cream
2 cups milk
1 teaspoon vanilla extract
2 tablespoons packed brown sugar

1 can (15 ounces) cream of coconut

2 tablespoons rum (optional) **or**
  1 teaspoon rum extract

1 package (12 ounces) semi-sweet chocolate pieces

Suggested Dippers: Assorted Pepperidge Farm® Cookies, Pepperidge Farm® Giant Goldfish® Grahams, whole strawberries, banana chunks, dried pineapple pieces **and/or** fresh pineapple chunks

Chocolate and Coconut Cream Fondue

START TO FINISH: 15 minutes

Prepping: 5 minutes
Cooking: 10 minutes

1. Stir the cream of coconut, rum and chocolate in a 2-quart saucepan. Heat over medium heat until the chocolate melts, stirring occasionally.

2. Pour the chocolate mixture into a fondue pot or slow cooker.

3. Serve warm with the *Suggested Dippers*.

Makes: 3 cups

Leftover Tip: Any remaining fondue can be used as an ice cream or dessert topping. Cover and refrigerate in an airtight container. Reheat in saucepot until warm.

I'm Dreamy for White Chocolate Fondue

START TO FINISH: 15 minutes

Prepping: 5 minutes
Cooking: 10 minutes

1. Stir the cream, liqueur and chocolate in a 1-quart saucepan. Heat over low heat until the chocolate melts, stirring occasionally.

2. Pour the chocolate mixture into a fondue pot or slow cooker.

3. Serve warm with the *Suggested Dippers*.

Makes 1½ cups

⅓ **cup heavy cream**
1 **tablespoon orange-flavored liqueur or ½ teaspoon orange extract**
1 **package (about 12 ounces) white chocolate pieces**

Suggested Dippers: Assorted Pepperidge Farm® Cookies, whole strawberries, banana chunks, dried pineapple pieces **and/or** fresh pineapple chunks

1 bag (5.1 ounces)
    Pepperidge Farm®
    Mini Chocolate Chunk
    Cookies, coarsely
    crumbled (about
    2 cups)
1 cup miniature
    marshmallows
    Vegetable cooking spray
3 cups semi-sweet
    chocolate pieces
    (18 ounces)
1 can (14 ounces)
    sweetened
    condensed milk
⅛ teaspoon salt
1 teaspoon vanilla extract

Sweet Treats

Super Chunky Fudge

START TO FINISH: 2 hours 25 minutes

Prepping: 15 minutes
Cooking: 10 minutes
Refrigerating: 2 hours

1 . Reserve ½ **cup** crumbled cookies and ¼ **cup** marshmallows. Line an 8-inch square baking pan with foil. Spray the foil with cooking spray. Heat the chocolate, milk and salt in a 2-quart saucepan over low heat until the chocolate melts, stirring often.

2. Remove the chocolate mixture from the heat and stir in remaining crumbled cookies, remaining marshmallows and vanilla. Spread the mixture evenly into the prepared pan. Press the reserved cookies and marshmallows into top of fudge.

3. Refrigerate for 2 hours or until firm. Remove fudge from pan and peel away foil. Cut into 16 squares. Cover with foil. Store in the refrigerator.

Makes: 2 pounds

Fishy Families

START TO FINISH: 36 minutes 15 seconds

Prepping: 5 minutes
Cooking: 1 minute 15 seconds
Refrigerating: 30 minutes

1. Line a baking sheet with waxed paper and set it aside. Place the chocolate in a microwavable bowl. Microwave on HIGH for 1 minute. Stir. Microwave at 15 second intervals, stirring after each, until the chocolate melts. Stir in the crackers to coat.

2. Scoop up the cracker mixture with a tablespoon and drop onto the prepared baking sheet. Sprinkle with the nonpareils. Repeat with the remaining cracker mixture and nonpareils.

3. Refrigerate for 30 minutes or until the mixture is firm. Store in the refrigerator.

Makes: 1 pound

1 package (12 ounces) semi-sweet chocolate pieces (2 cups)
2½ cups Pepperidge Farm® Pretzel Goldfish® Baked Snack Crackers
1 container (4 ounces) multi-colored nonpareils

CHOCOLATE PIECES

Sweet Treats

Bourbon Orange Chocolate Lady Dessert

2 fluid ounces
   (4 tablespoons)
   bourbon **or**
   orange juice
1 bag (7 ounces)
   Pepperidge Farm®
   Orange Milano®
   Distinctive Cookies,
   crushed
1 pint Godiva® Belgian
   Dark Chocolate Ice
   Cream, softened
Orange slices
Orange peel

START TO FINISH: 1 hour

Prepping: 15 minutes
Freezing: 45 minutes

1. Heat the bourbon in a 1-quart saucepan over high heat to a boil. Reduce the heat to low. Cook for 3 minutes. Remove from heat and let cool. Crush **3** of the cookies.

2. Mix the bourbon, ice cream and crushed cookies in a 1-quart bowl.

3. Freeze for 45 minutes or until the mixture is firm. Scoop into dessert dishes. Garnish with orange slices, orange peel and remaining whole cookies, if desired.

Makes: 4 servings

Cooking for a Crowd: Recipe may be doubled.

Sweet Treats

Candied Walnuts

START TO FINISH: 1 hour 15 minutes

Prepping: 10 minutes
Baking: 35 minutes
Cooling: 30 minutes

1. Beat the egg white in a small bowl with a fork until frothy. Add the walnuts and toss to coat.

2. Mix the sugar and cinnamon in a pie plate or shallow bowl. Using a slotted spoon, transfer the nuts in batches to the sugar mixture and toss to coat. Spoon the coated nuts onto a lightly greased or parchment paper-lined baking sheet.

3. Bake at 300°F. for 35 minutes or until lightly browned, stirring once after 15 minutes. Let cool on a wire rack. Break apart any clusters into bite-size pieces. Store in an airtight container for up to one week.

Makes: 1½ cups

Easy Substitution Tip: Substitute ground red pepper or a Creole seasoning blend for the cinnamon.

1 egg white
1 package (6 ounces) walnut halves (1½ cups)
¾ **cup sugar**
1 teaspoon ground cinnamon

Sweet Treats

2 packages (10 ounces **each**) Pepperidge Farm® Frozen Puff Pastry Shells
1 package (8 ounces) cream cheese, softened
1 tablespoon sugar
2 tablespoons orange juice
2 teaspoons grated orange peel
1 cup thawed frozen whipped topping
6 strawberries, cut in half
3 peeled orange slices, cut into quarters
1 kiwi, peeled and cut into 12 chunks
½ cup apricot preserves, warmed

Citrus Fruit Tartlets

START TO FINISH: 1 hour 15 minutes

Prepping: 30 minutes
Baking: 15 minutes
Cooling: 30 minutes

1. Heat the oven to 400°F. Bake and cool the pastry shells according to the package directions.

2. Beat the cream cheese, sugar, orange juice and orange peel in a medium bowl with an electric mixer on medium speed until smooth. Fold in the whipped topping.

3. Spoon about **3 tablespoons** cream cheese mixture into each shell. Divide the strawberries, oranges and kiwi fruit among the shells. Brush the preserves over the fruit. Serve immediately, or cover and refrigerate or up to 4 hours.

Makes: 12 servings

Time-Saving Tip: Cream cheese is easier to beat until smooth when it's softened first. Remove the wrapper and place the cheese on a microwavable plate. Microwave on HIGH for 15 seconds.

Mini Chocolate Cookie Cheesecakes

START TO FINISH: 3 hours 40 minutes

Prepping: 20 minutes
Baking: 20 minutes
Cooling: 1 hour
Refrigerating: 2 hours

1. Heat the oven to 350°F. Put the foil baking cups into 16 (2½-inch) muffin-pan cups or on a baking sheet. Place **2** cookies in the bottom of each cup and set aside. Cut the remaining cookies in half.

2. Beat the cream cheese, sugar, eggs and vanilla in a medium bowl with an electric mixer on medium speed until smooth. Spoon the cheese mixture into the baking cups filling each cup ¾ full. Insert **2** cookie halves, with the cut ends down, into the cheese mixture of each cup.

3. Bake for 20 minutes or until the centers are set. Cool the cheesecakes on a wire rack for 1 hour. Refrigerate the cheesecakes for at least 2 hours before serving.

Makes: 16 servings

16 Reynolds® Foil Baking
 Cups (2½-inch)
 2 packages (4.9 ounces
 each) Pepperidge
 Farm® Mini Milano®
 Distinctive Cookies
 2 packages (8 ounces
 each) cream cheese,
 softened
½ cup sugar
 2 eggs
½ teaspoon vanilla extract

Chocolate Cherry Ice Cream Cake

START TO FINISH: 2 hours 25 minutes

Prepping: 10 minutes
Freezing: 2 hours 15 minutes

1. Stand **10** of the cookies on their sides along the edge of a 9-inch springform pan, forming a ring. Coarsely chop the remaining cookies.

2. Spoon the black cherry ice cream into the pan and spread into an even layer. Spoon **1** jar of the chocolate sauce over the ice cream. Sprinkle with the coarsely chopped cookies. Freeze for 15 minutes.

3. Evenly spread the vanilla ice cream over the cookie layer. Pour the remaining chocolate sauce in the center, spreading into a circle to within 1 inch of the edge. Pipe the whipped cream around the top edge. Freeze for 2 hours more or until the mixture is firm. Place the cherries on top of the chocolate sauce just before serving.

Makes: 10 servings

Time-Saving Tip: The ice cream will be easier to spread when it's slightly softened. Let the ice cream sit at room temperature about 10 minutes before spooning onto the crust. Spread gently with a flexible spatula to make an even layer.

1 package (6 ounces) Pepperidge Farm® Milano® Distinctive Cookies
1 container (1.75 quarts) black cherry ice cream
2 jars (17 ounces **each**) chocolate ice cream sauce
1 container (1.75 quarts) vanilla ice cream
Sweetened whipped cream for garnish
Frozen pitted dark cherries, thawed for garnish

Southern Pecan Crisps

START TO FINISH: 1 hour 47 minutes

Thawing: 40 minutes
Prepping: 25 minutes
Baking: 12 minutes
Cooling: 30 minutes

1. Thaw the pastry sheet at room temperature for 40 minutes or until it's easy to handle. Heat the oven to 400°F. Mix the brown sugar and the pecans with the butter in a small bowl.

2. Unfold the pastry sheet on a lightly floured surface. Roll the sheet into a 15×12-inch rectangle. Cut the pastry into (20) 3-inch squares. Press the squares into bottoms of 3-inch muffin-pan cups. Place **1 heaping teaspoon** pecan mixture in the center of **each** cup.

3. Bake for 12 minutes or until golden. Remove the pastry from the pans and cool on a wire rack. Sprinkle the pastries with the confectioners' sugar before serving.

Makes: 20 pastries

½ of a 17.3 ounce package Pepperidge Farm® Frozen Puff Pastry Sheets (1 sheet)
½ cup packed brown sugar
⅓ cup pecan halves, chopped
2 tablespoons butter, melted
Confectioners' sugar

1 box (16 ounces) angel food cake mix
1¾ cups Diet V8 Splash® Berry Blend Juice
6 cups cut-up fresh strawberries, blueberries and raspberries
1½ cups thawed light whipped topping

Quick & Easy Berry Shortcakes

START TO FINISH: 2 hours 20 minutes

Prepping: 10 minutes
Baking: 40 minutes
Cooling: 1 hour 30 minutes

1. Heat the oven to 350°F. Prepare the cake mix according to the package directions, substituting juice for the water. Pour the batter into a 10-inch tube pan.

2. Bake for 40 minutes or until the top is golden brown and springs back when lightly touched with a finger. The cracks in the top of the cake should look dry. Invert the cake in the pan and hang upside down on a funnel or heatproof glass bottle for about 1½ hours to cool completely.

3. Loosen cake from pan with a metal spatula. Cut the cake into **24** slices. For each serving, place **1** cake slice on a serving plate, top with ¼ **cup** berries and **1 tablespoon** whipped topping, top with another cake slice, ¼ **cup** berries and **1 tablespoon** whipped topping. Repeat with remaining cake slices, berries and whipped topping.

Makes: 12 servings

Sweet Treats

Mandarin Orange Ginger Cream Puffs

START TO FINISH: 1 hour 5 minutes

Prepping: 20 minutes
Baking: 15 minutes
Cooling: 30 minutes

1. Heat the oven to 400°F. Bake and cool the pastry shells according to the package directions.

2. Prepare the pudding mix according to the package directions **except** use **1 cup** milk and add the ginger. Fold in the whipped cream.

3. Split the pastries into 2 layers. Place **4** orange segments on each bottom layer. Using a pastry bag fitted with a large fluted decorating tip, pipe ½ **cup** pudding mixture on each. Top with top layers and **3** orange segments. Serve immediately, or cover and refrigerate up to 4 hours. Just before serving, brush the jelly over the orange segments. Sift the sugar over the pastries. Top with orange peel. Garnish with berries and herbs as desired.

Makes: 6 servings

*For 1½ **cups** sweetened whipped cream, beat ¾ **cup** heavy cream, **2 tablespoons** sugar and ¼ **teaspoon** vanilla extract in a chilled medium bowl using an electric mixer at high speed until stiff peaks form.

1 package (10 ounces) Pepperidge Farm® Frozen Puff Pastry Shells
1 package (about 3½ ounces) vanilla instant pudding & pie filling mix
1 cup milk
½ teaspoon ground ginger
1½ cups sweetened whipped cream*
1 can (11 ounces) Mandarin orange segments, drained
2 tablespoons apple jelly, melted
Confectioners' sugar
Orange peel
Assorted fresh berries (raspberries, blackberries **and/or** blueberries)
Fresh herb leaves (thyme, lavender, rosemary **or** mint)

Beverages

Frosted Citrus Green Tea

2 bottles (16 fluid ounces each) Diet V8 Splash® Tropical Blend Juice (4 cups), chilled
4 cups strong brewed green tea*
Fresh mint sprigs (optional)
Lemon slices (optional)

START TO FINISH: 3 hours 30 minutes

Prepping: 2 hours
Freezing/Refrigerating: 1 hour 30 minutes

1. Pour **2 cups** juice into **1** ice cube tray. Freeze for 1 hour 30 minutes or until the mixture is frozen.

2. Mix the remaining juice and tea in an 8-cup measure. Refrigerate for at least 1 hour and 30 minutes.

3. Unmold the cubes from the tray and place 3 to 4 cubes in each of **6** tall glasses. Divide the tea mixture among the glasses. Serve with mint and lemon, if desired.

Makes: 6 servings

*__Strong brewed tea:__ Heat 4 cups of water in a 2-quart saucepan over high heat to a boil. Remove the pan from the heat. Add **8** tea bags and let them steep for 5 minutes. Remove the tea bags.

1 bottle (46 fluid ounces)
V8® 100% Vegetable
Juice
1 can (6 ounces) frozen
orange juice
concentrate
1½ cups plain **or** orange-
flavored seltzer water
Ice cubes

Orange Mist

START TO FINISH: 5 minutes

Prepping: 5 minutes

1. Stir the vegetable juice and orange juice in a large pitcher until the mixture is smooth.

2. Add the seltzer water.

3. Pour over ice-filled tall glasses.

Makes: 10 servings

Beverages

Jump Start Smoothie

START TO FINISH: 10 minutes

Prepping: 10 minutes

1. Put the juice, yogurt and strawberries in an electric blender container.
2. Cover and blend until smooth.
3. Serve immediately.

Makes: 4 servings

1 bottle (16 fluid ounces) V8 Splash® Orange Pineapple Juice (2 cups), chilled
1 cup vanilla lowfat yogurt
2 cups frozen whole strawberries or raspberries

1 bottle (64 fluid ounces) V8® 100% Vegetable Juice, chilled
1 container (64 fluid ounces) refrigerated lemonade
1 tablespoon Worcestershire sauce (optional)
2 lemons, thinly sliced
2 limes, thinly sliced
1 orange, thinly sliced
Ice cubes

Lemon Sangria Punch

START TO FINISH: 10 minutes

Prepping: 10 minutes

1. Stir the juice, lemonade and Worcestershire, if desired, lemons, limes and orange in an 8-quart punch bowl.

2. Serve immediately or refrigerate until serving time.

3. Pour over ice-filled tall glasses.

Makes: 20 servings

Beverages

Bellini Splash

START TO FINISH: 5 minutes

Prepping: 5 minutes

1. Stir the juice and nectar in a 1-cup measure.
2. Divide between 2 fluted champagne glasses. Pour in champagne.
3. Serve immediately.

Makes: 2 servings

Cooking for a Crowd: Recipe may be doubled or tripled.

½ **cup V8 Splash® Peach Lemonade or Mango Peach, chilled**
¼ **cup peach nectar, chilled**
1 **cup champagne, sparkling wine or sparkling cider, chilled**

1 bottle (16 fluid ounces) V8 Splash® Tropical Blend Juice (2 cups), chilled
1 pint orange or mango sherbet or vanilla ice cream
1 cup crushed ice
1 medium banana, sliced

Tropical Freeze

START TO FINISH: 10 minutes

Prepping: 10 minutes

1. Put the juice, sherbet, ice and banana in an electric blender container.
2. Cover and blend until it's smooth.
3. Serve immediately.

Makes: 4 servings

Beverages

Spicy Mary Martinis

START TO FINISH: 5 minutes

Prepping: 5 minutes

1. Put the juice, vodka, pepper sauce and ice in a cocktail shaker. Cover and shake until blended.

2. Strain into 2 chilled tall glasses rimmed with seasoned salt, if desired.

3. Serve with the celery.

Makes: 2 servings

2 cans (5.5 fluid ounces each) V8® Spicy Hot Vegetable Juice
3 fluid ounces (6 tablespoons) pepper-flavored vodka
Dash chipotle hot pepper sauce (or to taste)
2 cups ice cubes
Seasoned salt (optional)
2 stalks celery

1 can (5.5 fluid ounces)
V8® **or** Spicy Hot
Vegetable Juice
1½ fluid ounces
(3 tablespoons) vodka
1 teaspoon lemon juice
Dash Worcestershire
sauce
Dash hot pepper sauce
Ice cubes
1 stalk celery

Salsa Sipper

START TO FINISH: 5 minutes

Prepping: 5 minutes

1. Stir the juice, vodka, lemon juice, Worcestershire and hot pepper sauce in a 2-cup measure.

2. Pour into an ice-filled tall glass.

3. Serve with the celery.

Makes: 1 serving

Cooking for a Crowd: Recipe may be doubled or tripled.

Beverages

Russian Witches' Brew

START TO FINISH: 20 minutes

Prepping: 5 minutes
Cooking: 15 minutes

1. Stir the juice, tea, **3** cinnamon sticks and cloves in a 4-quart saucepot. Heat over medium-high heat to a boil. Reduce the heat to medium-low and cook for 10 minutes. Remove the cinnamon sticks and cloves.

2. Place remaining cinnamon sticks in 8 mugs and fill with juice mixture.

3. Serve immediately or keep it warm in the saucepot over very low heat.

Makes: 8 servings

*Strong brewed tea: Heat 4 cups of water in a 2-quart saucepan over high heat to a boil. Remove the pan from the heat. Add **8** tea bags and let them steep for 5 minutes. Remove the tea bags.

Cooking for a Crowd: Recipe may be doubled or tripled.

2 bottles (16 fluid ounces each) V8 Splash® Tropical Blend Juice (4 cups)
4 cups strong brewed tea*
11 cinnamon sticks
8 whole cloves

1 bottle (16 fluid ounces)
    V8® Splash Berry
    Blend Juice (2 cups)
2 fluid ounces (¼ cup) dark
    spiced **or** regular rum
½ teaspoon ground
    cinnamon
¼ teaspoon ground ginger
2 cinnamon sticks

Berry Rum Toddies

START TO FINISH: 10 minutes

Prepping/Cooking: 10 minutes

1. Heat the juice, rum, cinnamon and ginger in a 1-quart saucepan to a boil and cook for 5 minutes, stirring occasionally.

2. Pour the juice mixture into 2 mugs.

3. Serve with the cinnamon. Serve immediately.

Makes: 2 servings

Tropical Champagne Ice

START TO FINISH: 5 hours, 15 minutes

Prepping: 15 minutes
Freezing: 5 hours

1. Stir the juice, champagne and orange peel, if desired, in a 13×9×2-inch metal baking pan.

2. Cover and freeze for 5 hours or until frozen. After 2 hours, stir with a fork every hour.

3. Scoop **about ½ cup** champagne ice into a stemmed glass or dessert dish. Top with the fruit. Serve immediately. Cover and freeze any leftover ice. Let it stand at room temperature for 5 minutes to soften before scooping.

Makes: 18 servings

3 bottles (16 fluid ounces each) V8 Splash® Tropical Blend Juice, chilled
1 bottle (750 ml) champagne (3 cups), chilled
1 teaspoon grated orange peel (optional)
4½ cups cut-up fresh fruit (mango, papaya or pineapple)

Index

Index

Metric Conversion Chart

VOLUME MEASUREMENTS (dry)

1/8 teaspoon = 0.5 mL
1/4 teaspoon = 1 mL
1/2 teaspoon = 2 mL
3/4 teaspoon = 4 mL
1 teaspoon = 5 mL
1 tablespoon = 15 mL
2 tablespoons = 30 mL
1/4 cup = 60 mL
1/3 cup = 75 mL
1/2 cup = 125 mL
2/3 cup = 150 mL
3/4 cup = 175 mL
1 cup = 250 mL
2 cups = 1 pint = 500 mL
3 cups = 750 mL
4 cups = 1 quart = 1 L

VOLUME MEASUREMENTS (fluid)

1 fluid ounce (2 tablespoons) = 30 mL
4 fluid ounces (1/2 cup) = 125 mL
8 fluid ounces (1 cup) = 250 mL
12 fluid ounces (1 1/2 cups) = 375 mL
16 fluid ounces (2 cups) = 500 mL

WEIGHTS (mass)

1/2 ounce = 15 g
1 ounce = 30 g
3 ounces = 90 g
4 ounces = 120 g
8 ounces = 225 g
10 ounces = 285 g
12 ounces = 360 g
16 ounces = 1 pound = 450 g

DIMENSIONS

1/16 inch = 2 mm
1/8 inch = 3 mm
1/4 inch = 6 mm
1/2 inch = 1.5 cm
3/4 inch = 2 cm
1 inch = 2.5 cm

OVEN TEMPERATURES

250°F = 120°C
275°F = 140°C
300°F = 150°C
325°F = 160°C
350°F = 180°C
375°F = 190°C
400°F = 200°C
425°F = 220°C
450°F = 230°C

BAKING PAN SIZES

Utensil	Size in Inches/Quarts	Metric Volume	Size in Centimeters
Baking or Cake Pan (square or rectangular)	8×8×2	2 L	20×20×5
	9×9×2	2.5 L	23×23×5
	12×8×2	3 L	30×20×5
	13×9×2	3.5 L	33×23×5
Loaf Pan	8×4×3	1.5 L	20×10×7
	9×5×3	2 L	23×13×7
Round Layer Cake Pan	8×1½	1.2 L	20×4
	9×1½	1.5 L	23×4
Pie Plate	8×1¼	750 mL	20×3
	9×1¼	1 L	23×3
Baking Dish or Casserole	1 quart	1 L	—
	1½ quart	1.5 L	—
	2 quart	2 L	—

Metric Conversion Chart